Whence Came They?

Whence Came They?

Israel
Britain
and the
Restoration

BY VAUGHN E. HANSEN, PH.D.

Library of Congress
Card Catalog Number 93-74502

ISBN: 1-55517-429-9

Published and Distributed by:
925 North Main, Springville, UT 84663 • 801/489-4084

CFI   Publishing and
       Distribution Since 1986
Cedar Fort, Incorporated
CFI Distribution • CFI Books • Council Press • Bonneville Books

Cover Design by Lyle Mortimer
Page Layout and Design by Brian Carter
Lithographed in the United States of America

CONTENTS

Chapter Six

Chapter Seven

Figures

TABLES

ACKNOWLEDGMENTS

Foremost, I would like to recognize and acknowledge the revelation and guidance given by a loving Heavenly Father to searchers after truth. Prophets have recorded and authors have extensively researched and made available pertinent information regarding God's master plan for the growth and salvation of mankind. One of the central themes of the plan has been the distinctive role and destiny of Israel.

The British Israel World Federation and their associates in Canada and the United States of America have, with their publications, effectively drawn a clearer image of Israel's contributions, whereabouts, and destiny. Mr. R. B. H. Hall of that organization has kindly and graciously assisted the author in assembling pertinent information. Reverend Robert Griffith, chaplain for the British Israel World Federation and Imperial Grand Chaplain of British Druids, has both in personal discussion and written documents conveyed essential knowledge. Both Mr. Hall and Reverend Griffith were truly gracious, kind and Christlike.

Appreciation goes to the authors of relevant publications and their publishers for graciously extending permission to quote from their work. A reply from one expresses the purposes of all: "Yours in the service of the King of Kings."

Dr. David Wood, Karen Hansen, Helen Burton, and

Paul Hansen have kindly assisted in the preparation of the manuscript. Dr. David Gailey, Dr. F. Richard Hauck, Kenneth and Cheryl North, LeR Burton, John Piercey, Audrey Nelson and Dr. Lindon Beales have reviewed the manuscript and have offered helpful suggestions. The publisher, Lyle Mortimer, and excellent editorial assistance of Dr. Frances Anne Smeath have made it possible to share with others a reminder of the heritage that is ours as Children of Israel.

The heritage bequeathed by my ancestors is most precious. My sincere desire is that the readers of this book will cherish and honor their ancestral heritage.

Words cannot express my gratitude to Donell, my eternal companion and devoted wife, for her constant support. I am grateful to our ten children for their love, their support, and their adherence to righteousness.

INTRODUCTION:

GOALS AND PREMISES

Whence Came They? Israel, Britian and the Restoration, has grown out of my intense desire to learn from whence came the strength, the leadership, the character, and the nobility that I believe was so much a part of my ancestors. Such characteristics must be built upon a solid foundation. They do not just happen. Who were these British people that seem to have had such a positive impact upon the world?

As I sought answers, my thoughts converged upon the England of my ancestors (Figure 1). What I discovered was exciting. I began to see patterns which suggested that early Britons were noble Hebrews and Israelites, with a strong culture and a firm religious belief. This brought me a much keener appreciation for my British ancestry. In this book I hope to present the legends and traditions which form this pattern. I hope that my readers will find these stories, covering nearly 4500 years, exciting and rewarding.

Principal emphasis herein will be upon early Britons, but much that is discussed will also pertain to cousins in the Scandinavian countries and the Netherlands and to other scattered remnants mainly in northern Europe. The concept that large numbers of Israelite descendants can be found in western Russia will also be discussed.

This book has been prepared to share exciting, often little-known information, in the hope that not only will the reader find a deeper appreciation for his or her own ancestry and heritage, but also in the hope that readers might come to cherish the knowledge of who they are. Knowledge can emphasize responsibility and provide a more solid foundation for the increasingly severe moral and spiritual storms that lie ahead. Vision beyond the storm to a brighter day can bring confidence and the resolve to endure.

Figure 1
British Isles

The following pages will consider the panorama of Israel's dispersion and migrations to the "Isles of the Sea." We will look at struggles for survival, the source of strength to resist aggression, and the impacts of prophets and inspired leaders. Distinctive emblems belonging to each tribe of Israel will be identified. Leading roles now being played by specific tribes of Israel and sequential steps in the Gathering of Israel will also be discussed.

God's covenant Israel has been led to places of refuge, protected and defended, given prophetic guidance, and assigned a key role in the final hours of the restoration, the gathering and the ushering in of the millennium. This book is based on the premise that we are Israelites with a royal heritage, a choice generation. I believe this is a fact we need to recognize.

This book is not intended to be an exhaustive academic reference, but rather a window through which the reader can view the foggy past with a desire to learn more of the priceless heritage left by those who have preceded us. As data has accumulated, the patterns which this book will present have become more recognizable, and the historic panorama has become increasingly beautiful.

Many individuals, recent and historic, have written extensively on these subjects—their data has been used as a resource for this book. For example, more than a hundred years ago, in 1880, the Reverend W. H. Pool published in New York a lecture entitled History, the True Key to Prophecy in Which the Saxon Race is Shown to be the Lost Tribe of Israel (Ref. 27). To support his claim, 58 references were cited, one of which was Swiss historian

John Von Muller. In a life-long study, Von Muller extract-
ed information from 1733 authors. Several authors quoted herein have referred to from 30 to 75 additional writers. But Isabel Hill Elder (Ref. 12) has been the most
exhaustive, quoting from more than 380 published
sources including documents in several languages.

Thus the synopsis to follow is derived from the studies
of many authors. My objective is to bring to the reader,
from these numerous sources, a picture of the past that
may help not only to identify significant past events but
also to focus more clearly on the future. The common
thread throughout is the premise that a unique role has
been played by our Israelite ancestors, and that each of
us also has a role to play as the present-day generation of
the Children of Israel.

As Israelite migrations are discussed, it is important
to remember that other groups of people were also present. This document is a review of one select group only,
their journeys to and their impact upon Great Britain.

Written records for some periods are scarce. Evidence
from archaeology and other scientific endeavors must
then be sought to clarify certain issues. As research continues, pertinent information continues to come forth.

Skeptics may criticize legends as being unsubstantiat-
ed, and it is true that early oral histories and first written
records are often fragmentary. Taken alone, such legends
and records may be justifiably questioned. However, truth
becomes more evident when fragments from many
sources fit together into a consistent pattern. Separate
pieces of a jigsaw puzzle viewed alone often do not appear

to belong together. But when piece after piece of the puzzle is studied and placed in the proper position, a grand and often beautiful picture emerges. And so it is with the contents of this book—each separate piece of information can be seen as part of a consistent and glorious picture. Each piece has the capability of adding to the whole.

I urge the reader to proceed with an open mind and withhold judgment until the fragments presented here are compiled into a whole image. Bacon in his Advancement of Learning states that...

> Out of monuments, names, proverbs, traditions, private records and evidences, fragments of stories, passages of books and the like, we do save and recover somewhat from the deluge of time.

My sincere desire is that with an understanding of the illustrious, if often stormy past of our ancestors, we will gain increased reverence for those who preceded and gave us so much. Hopefully, with an increased appreciation for the past, we might sense an increased responsibility to those who come after us. Basically, the following pages have been prepared that, as an ancient prophet said, "When ye remember their works ye may know that they were good." (Helaman 5:6)

"We are given the names of our righteous parents that we may remember their works and pattern our lives upon theirs." (Ref. 5:333)

SELECTED CHRONOLOGY

A selected chronology follows, as a handy reference tool to suggest a possible sequence for the historical events being discussed in the book. Dates in brackets are based only on legend or tradition, and should not be taken as factual merely by being included in the chronology. Dates without brackets can be validated by independent sources and are thus to be considered more factual. Among many other works, The Timetables of History: A Horizontal Linkage of People and Events, by Bernard Grun, was used extensively in verifying this chronology.

DATE...	EVENT...
[unknown]	Expulsion from the Garden of Eden
[unknown]	Life of Adam
[unknown]	Life of Enoch
[unknown]	City of Enoch translated
[unknown]	Life of Noah
[unknown]	The Flood
[unknown]	Tower of Babel
[unknown]	Life of Eber (progenitor of Hebrews)
[ca. 2052-1877 B.C.]	Life of Abraham
[ca. 2300-1500 B.C.]	Development of Stonehenge
[ca. 1892-1745 B.C.]	Life of Jacob (renamed Israel)
[ca. 1801-1691 B.C.]	Life of Joseph, son of Jacob

[ca. 1800 B.C.]	Hu Gadarn Husicion reputedly migrates to Britain
[ca. 1600 B.C.]	Descendants of Zarah-Judah leave Egypt and migrate to Spain
[ca. 1486 B.C.]	The Exodus of the Tribes of Israel from Egypt
[ca. 1411-1407 B.C.]	Tribes of Israel invade Canaan
[ca. 1185 B.C.]	Trojan Empire is destroyed
[ca. 1100 B.C.]	The legendary Brutus of Troy founds London
[ca. 967 B.C.]	Solomon's Temple is started
[ca. 922 B.C.]	Tribes of Israel are divided into two rival kingdoms
[ca. 721, 715, 677 B.C.]	Northern Kingdom of Israel invaded and taken captive by Assyrians
[ca. 612 B.C.]	Babylon conquers Assyrian Empire
[ca. 600 B.C.]	The prophet Lehi and family leaves Jerusalem
[ca. 581 B.C.]	Southern Kingdom of Israel invaded, Jerusalem destroyed, and Judah taken captive by Babylonians
[ca. post-586 B.C.]	The prophet Jeremiah flees to Egypt
536 B.C.	Cyrus the Great of Persia, conqueror of Babylon, allows Jews to return to Jerusalem
55 B.C.	Julius Caesar invades England
0	BIRTH OF JESUS CHRIST
[ca. 12-30 A.D.]	Jesus said to have visited England with Joseph of Arimathaea
33 A.D.	Jesus Christ is crucified
[ca. 36 A.D.]	By tradition, Joseph of Arimethaea,Mary

	the mother of Jesus, and eleven others are cast adrift in the Mediterranean Sea
[ca. 37 A.D.]	Traditional date that Joseph of Arimethaea and Mary arrive in England
43 A.D.	Roman legions invade England
[ca. 48 A.D.]	Traditional death date of Mary the mother of Jesus in England
53 A.D.	Romans obtain a foothold in England
[ca. 56 A.D.]	Traditional date of Paul the Apostle's first mission to England
70 A.D.	Jerusalem destroyed by Romans; the Jews dispersed
[ca. 82 A.D.]	Traditional death date of Joseph of Arimethaea in England
180 A.D.	Romans, defeated in Scotland, retire to Hadrian's Wall
290 A.D.	Infamous Diocletian persecutions begin
446-501 A.D.	Anglo-Saxon invasions of Britain
[ca. 501 A.D.]	Posterity of Zarah-Judah migrates to western Scotland
[ca. 537 A.D.]	Traditional death date of King Arthur
602 A.D.	St. Augustine of Canterbury founds the archiepiscopal see of Canterbury
1066 A.D.	William of Normandy conquers England
1184 A.D.	Great fire at Glastonbury destroys the abbey
1328 A.D.	Treaty of Edinburgh / Northampton ratifies Scotland's independence from England
ca. 1380-1384 A.D.	John Wycliffe attacks Catholic practices and doctrine and translates the Vulgate Bible

By 1500 A.D.	Catholicism firmly established in south ern Ireland and southeastern England; Protestantism begins to emerge in Europe
1522 A.D.	Martin Luther translates New Testament
1525 A.D.	William Tyndale's New Testament translation is published
1536 A.D.	Church of England is established by King Henry VIII
1588 A.D.	Spanish Armada is defeated by British fleet
1611 A.D.	King James Version of The Holy Bible is printed
Early 1600s	Baptist faith emerges
1738 A.D.	Methodist faith emerges
1776 A.D.	America declares independence from Britain
1815 A.D.	Wellington defeats Napoleon at Waterloo
1830 A.D.	The Church of Jesus Christ of Latter-day Saints is organized (the Mormons)
1837 A.D.	First LDS missionaries arrive in England
1914 A.D.	World War I begins
1917 A.D.	Jerusalem is liberated from the Turks
1936 A.D.	Hitler forms the Axis with Italy
1948 A.D.	Palestine, by act of the U.N., becomes the Jewish state of Israel

CHAPTER ONE

EFFORTS TO DESTROY A FORTRESS FOR CHRISTIANITY

B efore we proceed to a discussion of early Hebrew and Israelite migrations to Britain, we will review in this chapter the intense. efforts throughout recorded history to destroy the Christian fortress. In Chapter 2, the source of strength to resist these aggressions will be considered. Early migrations, Israel's identifying tribal emblems and individuals having a pronounced impact on the issues will then be discussed. Points concerning the restoration of the gospel and God's covenant Israel will complete the book.

To begin this review, consider George N. Wilson's searching question:

> WHY have the inhabitants of these Islands [Britain] been so favored and protected over the centuries? This favour and protection at times of extreme national peril (The Armada, Dunkirk, the Battle of Britain, etc.) can only be described as "divine".... WHY? (Ref. 36:1)

One possible answer is that Lucifer (the adversary of God's plan of salvation), recognizing the strength and the destiny of the inhabitants of the British Isles, has always used and is still using every means available to defeat the work of the British descendants of the House of Israel, requiring a corresponding outpouring of the spirit on their behalf.

Times of extreme peril for Britain (and Israel) have lasted over two thousand years and continue today. Britain's size and location would seem to make her an easy target, yet she has withstood all external forces. Roman invasions lasted many years. The Spanish, especially during the tense period of the Spanish Armada, and the French under Napoleon did all in their power to conquer Britain. The invasion and submission of England was a central goal of Germany's expansionist policies which culminated in two World Wars. Even today, some believe that European interests are attempting to subjugate Britain through economic and political domination.

ROMAN INVASIONS

On August 5th, 55 B.C., Julius Caesar invaded southern England. He advanced only seven miles and lost the battle. He invaded again nine months later, advanced 70 miles, but then signed a treaty and withdrew all his forces from England. His great Roman legions could not triumph. The Emperor Caligula is quoted as having exclaimed "Let us, my comrades, leave these Britons unmolested. To war beyond nature is not courage, but impiety." (Ref. 1:49)

EXTERMINATE THE CHRISTIANS

Within nine years after the crucifixion of Christ,
Christianity had gained such a following in Britain that
Claudius, Emperor of the Romans, planned a campaign of
genocide against them. George F. Jowett discusses the
significance of this:

> In the year 42 A.D. Claudius, Emperor of the
> Romans, issued the fateful decree to destroy Christian
> Britain, man, woman and child, and its great institutions
> and burn its libraries. To this purpose Claudius equipped
> the largest and most efficient army ever sent by Rome to
> conquer a foe and led by its most able generals. In this
> edict, Claudius proclaimed in the Roman Senate that
> acceptance of the Druidic or Christian faith was a capital
> offence, punishable by death by the sword, the torture
> chamber, or to be cast to the devouring lions in the arena
> of the Colosseum. It is interesting to note that this ruling
> also included "any person descended from David." This
> meant the Jew, making no exceptions as to whether he be
> a converted Jew or one holding to the orthodox Judean
> faith.
>
> Further to seek to inflame the populace against
> Christian and Jew, the Romans were the first to create
> the false slander that Christian and Jew alike practiced
> human sacrifice in their religion. They knew better. They
> knew that the burnt offerings of Judean and Druid were
> animals, chiefly sheep, goats and doves. The Romans
> spread the ridiculous propaganda that the Jews devoured
> Gentile babies.
>
> Extermination of Britain and all that was Christian

was a Roman obsession. (Refs. 18: 89, 91, 93)

The historian Tacitus states that from 43 to 86 A.D. (43 long years) the Romans fought 60 major battles on British soil. Jowett says of this:

> Looking back on the pages of those bloodstained years the heart recoils in horror at the savagery, murder, massacre, rape and destruction inflicted upon the inhabitants and the land of the Sacred Isle. The Romans, who had ground so many nations under their despotic heel, looked upon all other nations with scorn as inferiors, labeling every enemy as barbarian, no matter how magnificent their culture. The records attest to the indisputable fact that the Romans of all people were the most barbarous and brutal in history. (Ref. 18:92-93)

The Romans, with their best legions, were able to obtain a foothold in Britain only after 10 years of incessant warfare and betrayal. They were never able to penetrate Wales and Scotland or the legendary sacred Isle of Avalon on the west coast. The significance of this isle will be discussed in detail in Chapter 5.

DIOCLETIAN PERSECUTIONS

Jowett further explains:

> The infamous Diocletian held the reins at Rome and on his orders began what is often described as the worst persecution of the Christians in the year A.D. 290. In his

Edict, he ordered churches to be pulled down, the sacred scriptures to be gathered together and burnt, along with other Christian literature on which they could lay their hands. Libraries, schools of learning and private homes were equally destroyed. ... No Christian was spared regardless of age or sex. Even the babes in arms of Christian parents were cruelly destroyed.

The Diocletian persecution reached Britain, A.D. 300, where again the Romans sought to destroy Christianity at its source. The Emperor poured a huge army into Britain. However, before victory crowned the British armies, the Romans had inflicted great destruction, levelling churches, universities and libraries, and sacking towns. The slaughter was terrific, totalling a list of British martyrs that far exceeded the total inflicted by all the former persecutions combined. (Refs. 18: 215,216)

Britain is the only nation in the history ever attacked by the full might of another powerful people in an effort to purge Christianity off the face of the earth. ... From the Claudian to the Diocletian persecution, extermination of Britain and all that was Christian was a Roman obsession. (Ref. 18:93)

Some research points to the probability that, for centuries, Rome systematically destroyed British libraries and records that would attest to the spiritual and physical strength that enabled the British to resist the onslaught of foreign invasions. This viewpoint sees Roman historians as rewriters of history, portraying Rome as the conveyor of civilization to the Isles of the Sea, and portraying the British as barbarians who sacrificed humans during their religious ceremonies at

Stonehenge. The concept of the Roman as civilized and the early Briton as barbaric is still much in vogue among historians and museum curators today. Yet, careful searches of Vatican records and archaeological excavations, for instance, are showing the true and noble characteristics of early Britons. These characteristics will be discussed in later chapters of the book.

EARLY CATHOLIC CHURCH

About 600 A.D., St. Augustine of Canterbury (not to be confused with St. Augustine, author of The City of God), became the first Roman Bishop in England. He made a strong effort to bring the Christian churches in Britain under the domination and leadership of Rome. Legend and tradition speak of Christian entities existing in Britain since the time of Christ's apostles. These entities had maintained their beliefs and ecclesiastical leadership in a much more pure form than had Rome. Hence, the British saw Augustine's efforts as an infringement of their liberties, and they recognized many of the beliefs and practices of the Roman Catholic Church as a departure from the doctrines of Christ. Elder elaborates on the rejection of St. Augustine's efforts:

> Britons told Augustine they would not be subject to
> him, nor allow him to pervert the ancient laws of their
> Church. This was their resolution and they were as good
> as their word, for they maintained the liberty of their
> Church for five hundred years after his time, and were

the last of all the Churches of Europe to give up their power to Rome.

The Christians of Britain could never understand why the Church of Rome, because she professed certain truths, should arrogate spiritual despotism over all who had the same. When Augustine demanded of Dionoth, Abbot of Bangor Iscoed, or Bangor-on-Dee, that he acknowledge the authority of the Bishop of Rome, the reply of the Briton was a memorable one: "We desire to love all men, but he whom you call 'Pope' is not entitled to style himself the 'father of fathers' and the only submission we can render him is that which we owe to every Christian." (Ref. 12:124-125)

By 1500 A.D., Catholicism had established itself quite firmly in southern Ireland and in southeastern and central England. The Catholic Church had acquired extensive land holdings and considerable wealth.

RISE OF PROTESTANTISM

In the sixteenth century, King Henry VIII married Catherine of Aragon who gave him a daughter, Mary, but no son. When the Pope refused to annul the marriage, Henry broke with Rome and established the Church of England by 1536, abolishing papal jurisdiction by Act of Parliament. He confiscated the Catholic Church's assets and greatly reduced its political influence.

Henry's second marriage, to Anne Boleyn, produced another daughter, Elizabeth. Jane Seymour, his third

wife, gave him his long-awaited son, Edward, who suc-
ceeded his father to the throne. After young King
Edward's death, Henry's daughter Mary I became queen
in 1553 A.D. She reestablished the supremacy of the
Catholic Church and married Philip, son of the emperor
of Spain, who was devotedly Catholic. Her intense persecution of Protestants, including burning at the stake
members of the Protestant clergy, earned her the name
"Bloody Mary." Upon her death, her half-sister, Elizabeth
I, a strong Protestant, became queen, reigning from 1558
to 1603.

In 1560 A.D. the Netherlands rebelled against their
overlord, King Philip II of Spain. The Pope regarded the
printing press and its support of the rebellion as a threat.
Consequently a large Spanish army occupied the
Netherlands to quell the rebellion and to destroy the
press. Ruthless brutality followed in some areas with a
reign of terror and the charge to kill every thing that
moved. The rebellion was quelled in the Netherlands, but
across the channel in Britain the press and Protestantism
continued to gain strength under the reign of Queen
Elizabeth. Some historians have stated their opinion that
the printing press shattered the power of Catholicism.

Conflict between Protestants and Catholics was also
rampant in France in the 1500s. In addition, after the
death of her husband Francis II (King of France), Mary
Stewart left France and went to Scotland to succeed her
late father, King James V of Scotland. As Queen of
Scotland and a devout Catholic, Mary Stewart fostered
Catholic factions against the strongly-Protestant clan

nobility. Following palace intrigues and civic rebellion, she was forced to abdicate and later fled to England, where she was put under perpetual house arrest—in effect, imprisoned—by Elizabeth, who recognized Mary as a focus of Catholic unrest, dangerous to England's political stability. Even from her closely guarded seclusion, Mary repeatedly plotted to assassinate Elizabeth I in an effort to replace her as Queen of England and reestablish Catholicism as the state religion. Mary was finally beheaded by Elizabeth in 1587 A.D. This and the defeat of the Spanish Armada the following year firmly entrenched Protestantism in England and Scotland.

SPANISH ARMADA

Philip II of Spain tried for years, using every means available short of open war, to overthrow Elizabeth, the champion of Protestantism. Elizabeth, although anxious to avoid war, knew that her life and England's social and economic future depended upon successfully opposing Philip.

In 1588, Philip II assembled an armada of 130-odd ships with an on-board army of some 20,000 soldiers and 8,000 mariners, supported by a ground army of 30,000, based in France across the channel at Calais. With these forces, he hoped to eliminate Elizabeth, crush Protestantism, and reestablish Catholicism in England, as well as protect Spain's position as the economic and cultural center of Europe. The Spanish Armada was to rendezvous with the ground army at Calais, defeat the English fleet in the channel, invade England, and strike overland in a massive campaign. Philip II believed England lacked the capacity to successfully resist.

On the 7th of August at midnight, while the Armada was anchored at Calais preparing to board Philip's ground troops, the English sent eight flaming boats between 90 and 200 tons each into the Spanish fleet. The Spanish broke anchor to avoid the fireships, in some cases cutting their anchor lines and colliding with their own ships in their haste to escape the flames. (Ref. 39:112-114) By full morning, the English navy attacked the scattering ships of the Armada, harrying them up the channel and inflicting heavy damage on some of the Spanish vessels. By afternoon, further good fortune came to the English in the form of a strong westerly squall that forced the Spanish to break formation and run before it. Philip's plans for linking up with the waiting army at Calais became impossible.

The Spanish not only had to abandon the invasion of England, but sail north around Scotland and then back down the west coast of the British Isles to reach home. Dysentery, disease, heavy gales, bitter cold and ship-wrecks off the Irish coast inflicted heavy losses on the fleet and the men. Only half the Armada returned to Spain. With this defeat, Spain's power to challenge Protestantism was effectively broken.

The destruction of the Spanish Armada was and still is recognized by England as an act of divine providence. The defeat was epoch-making, preserving the new social and political fabric which the Reformation had woven, and certainly saving England from a Spanish campaign on her soil.

NAPOLEON

The next major assault on England and Protestantism was by Napoleon. Lord Nelson's naval victory off Cape Trafalgar in 1805 eliminated Napoleon's chance to cross the sea and invade England. Finally, the Duke of Wellington, leader of the British army, defeated Napoleon at Waterloo in 1815, where Wellington was assisted by the timely arrival of the Prussians at a critical moment in the battle. Once again Britain had survived an attack on its sovereignty.

TWO WORLD WARS

From 1914 to 1918, Europe was devastated by a new, even more gigantic military struggle. Germany and Austria's aggressions resulted in terrible loss of life and destruction of natural resources, and threatened the very survival of world democracy. America entered the war on April 6, 1917, joining Britain and her allies, and helping to bring about a decisive victory, but only a short-lived peace.

In 1936, only 18 years after the armistice of 1918, Germany again moved aggressively into neighboring nations. The conflict rapidly spread world-wide. France surrendered to Germany in 1940, but the successful withdrawal of surviving British forces from the beaches at Dunkirk under heavy enemy fire prevented England's fall as well. Under the subsequent intense war for domination of the skies over England, the British miraculously held. Japan entered the conflict by attacking Pearl Harbor in 1941, which again brought America into the world-wide conflict. Britain, her colonies, and the United States fought together and, in 1945, finally overcame the menace.

ON-GOING OPPOSITION

These examples suggest that for 2,000 years, crucial attacks against Britain have occurred, noticeably from the Romans, the early Catholic Church in Italy, the Spanish Empire, Napoleon, and two world wars. It is the premise of this book that the leadership of Britain over many centuries has been the posterity of the House of Israel, and that the adversary has tried continually to destroy that leadership. If this is true, can we expect any less opposition from Satan in the future? In all probability the struggle will not diminish, but intensify.

CHAPTER TWO

WHENCE CAME THE STRENGTH TO RESIST AGGRESSION

Some historians say that Rome was the early bringer of civilization, while the rest of Europe was inhabited by "barbarians." If Rome conquered those nations, why could it not conquer the British?

Information contained herein is presented to help dispel erroneous beliefs that Britain was uncivilized compared with Rome, that Rome brought Christianity to Britain, or that the Druids in England were a mischievous sect conducting human sacrifice. I believe time will prove it true, rather, that the early inhabitants of Britain and parts of northern Europe were noble, god-fearing Israelites, a favored people. This chapter will describe conditions in Britain and the capacity that existed there to resist the aggression which history appears to prove. Subsequent chapters will describe legendary groups and traditional individuals who made major contributions to Britain's internal strength.

ANCIENT BRITAIN

Citing many sources, Isabel Hill Elder describes early Britain:

> Britain was, in fact, from at least 900 B.C. to the Roman invasion, the manufacturing centre of the world. [T]he Phoenicians ... had an established trade with Britain before the Trojan war, 1190 B.C. Admiral Himilco of Carthage, who visited Britain about the sixth century B.C. to explore the "outer parts of Europe", records that the Britons were a "powerful race, proud spirited, effectively skillful in art, and constantly busy with the cares of trade." (Ref. 12:29-30)
>
> Nor was Ireland less forward than Britain, for from ancient Greek records it would appear that trade routes both by sea and land existed in these very early times, the latter route being across Europe through the territories of the Scythians. A most curious belief of the Greeks was that the inspiration which led to the institution of the Olympic Games was derived from the observance of ancient Irish festivities. (Ref. 12:30)
>
> The Britons were renowned for their athletic form, for the great strength of their bodies, and for swiftness of foot. Clean-shaven, save for long moustaches, with fair skins and fair hair, they were a fine, manly race; of great height (Strabo tells us that British youths were six inches taller than the tallest man in Rome) and powerfully built. They excelled in running, swimming, wrestling, climbing and in all kinds of bodily exercise.... Bravery, fidelity to their word, manly independence, love of their national free institutions, and hatred of every pollution and meanness were their notable characteristics. (Ref. 12:18)

Tacitus tells us the northern Britons were well trained and armed for war. In the battle field they formed themselves into battalions; and soldiers were armed with huge swords and small shields called "short targets;" they had chariots and cavalry, and carried darts which they hurled in showers on the enemy. Magnificent as horseman, with their charges gaily caparisoned, they presented a splendid spectacle when prepared for battle. The cumulative evidence is of a people numerous, brave and energetic. (Ref. 12:18)

That Britain had a[n] indigenous system of law centuries before the Christian era is abundantly clear from the ancient histories of our islands. The lawgiver, Molmutus, 450 B.C., based his laws on the code of Brutus, 1100 B.C. (Ref. 12:22)

In these early times Britain was a wealthy country, with fine cities, a well-organized national life, and an educated and civilized people. The so-called Roman roads in Britain were constructed centuries before the Romans came to these islands. (Ref 12:26)

The British have been from all time a people apart, characterized by independence, justice and a love of religion. (Ref. 12:19)

The British, before the arrival of Julius Caesar, were, in all probability, among the most highly educated people on the earth at that time and, as regards scientific research, surpassed both the Greeks and the Romans—a fact testified to by both Greek and Roman writers themselves. (Ref. 12:20)

To these early Britons we owe what we prize most— freedom, knowledge and a higher sense of right and wrong. This goodly heritage comes to us neither from a Roman conquest nor through Roman influence. (Ref. 12:49)

Diodorus Siculus [a Roman historian], in 60 B.C., states "The Britons live in the same manner as the ancients did; they fight in chariots as the ancient heroes of Greece are said to have done in the Trojan wars.... They are plain and upright in their dealings, and far from the craft and subtlety of our countrymen.... The island is very populous.... The Celts never shut the doors of their houses; they invite strangers to their feasts, and when all is over ask who they are and what is their business." (Ref. 12:27)

Early Britons were skilled workers in pottery, turnery, smelting, glasswork, and enameling. They mined copper, iron, lead, silver, gold, and tin. (Ref. 12:31)

Over the centuries, Celts, Gaels, Anglo-Saxons, Danes and Normans invaded and colonized Britain. I believe these invaders will also eventually be revealed as primarily Israelite descendants completing a long migration from their ancient land. A more detailed discussion of these points will follow later.

James H. Anderson's comments from his book God's Covenant Race are pertinent:

It has grown to be a maxim among students of history that "as to Rome all ancient history converges, so from Rome all modern history begins." That was the effort of the Roman Catholic world-power to obscure knowledge outside of itself as the source. The modern prevalent opinion that "British history begins with Julius Caesar" does not represent the fact. The prophet Jeremiah (25:22), 606 B.C., mentions "the kings of the isles which are beyond the sea"—the Mediteranian [sic]—referring to the British Isles. These were the "isles afar off" of both the prophets Isaiah and Jeremiah. Tin for the temple of Solomon came from Cornwall in England, and from Spain. Herodotus, 450 B.C., refers to Britain as the Tin Islands. ... Aristotle [about 400 B.C.] tells of the "two islands beyond the Pillars of Hercules (Gibraltar) called British." An ancient map of the time of Strabo, 50 B.C., depicts Britannia and adjacent islands. Five hundred years before the opening of the Christian era, Tara, twenty-five miles northwest of Dublin, Ireland, was a great seat of learning. (Ref. 1:47)

It was not barbarians, in the modern use of the word, who twice signally defeated the Roman legions, compelling Caesar on his second expedition into Britain, to withdraw across the Strait of Dover on September 25, B.C. 54, leaving not a Roman soldier behind.... (Ref. 1:49)

It is common to assume, as a result of the transmutation of Roman war propaganda into history, that the early British were aboriginal savages contributing nothing to culture or religion, and that Rome brought culture, government, roads and architecture to these desolate far-off isles of the sea. On the contrary, more than 1500 years before Rome, a highly civilized and literate race existed in Britain. I believe they were Israelites who migrated to the isles where they could live in peace and worship God as directed by ancient prophets.

EARLY BRITISH CHURCH

Christianity as a church may have been born very early in Britain. It was established, tradition says, by Christ's disciples who came shortly after the crucifixion, building upon the foundation of much-earlier Hebrew prophets. St. Augustine of Canterbury and others from Rome established the Catholic Church in England some five hundred years later, ca. 600 A.D.

Anderson (see Ref. 1: 52,53) quotes several Anglo-Saxon histories, attesting to the existence of Christianity in Britain long before the Roman Catholic Church established churches in Britain. These quotations are included as evidence of the source of moral strength to resist aggression.

> Robert Parsons, the Jesuit, in his Three Conversions of England, Vol. 1, page 15, makes this statement: "It seems nearest the truth the British church was originally planted by Grecian teachers, such as came from the east, and not by Romans."
>
> Sabellius, Book 7, c. 6, says: "Christianity was privately confessed elsewhere, but the first nation that proclaimed it as their religion, and called itself Christian after the name of Christ, was Britain."
>
> Publius Discipulus writes: "The church of Avalon [Glastonbury, England] no other hands than those of the disciples of the Lord themselves built."
>
> Archbishop Ussher relates: "The mother church of the British Isles is the church in Insulla Avallonia, called by the Saxons, Glaston."

Recent excavations [have been made] at the church of
St. Peter-upon-Cornhill, one of the older of London's
church buildings, the present structure having been built
in 1680 upon the site where an earlier church building
was destroyed by fire, having uncovered a brass tablet
telling that the older building was erected in 179 A.D. by
"Lucius, the first Christian king of this land, then called
Britaine."

Eusebius, A.D. 320, in Book 3, says: "The apostles
passed beyond the ocean to the isles called the British
Isles."

Chrysostom, 402 A.D., says: "The British Isles which
are beyond the sea, and which lie in the ocean, have
received the virtue of the Word. Churches are there
founded and altars erected."

Tertullian, 1192 A.D., says: "Regions in Britain which
have never been penetrated by the Roman arms have
received the religion of Christ."

The subsequent growth of Protestantism in Britain
and the several translations of The Bible into English
provided individuals with additional strength by increas-
ing religious freedom and understanding. The statement
in the preface of the King James translation clearly identifies its purpose: "...to make God's holy truth to be yet
more and more known unto the people...."

CENTERS OF LEARNING

Britain had developed a strong and unique culture by
the time of Caesar. Ancient Britons considered their man-

ufacture of glass and pottery unsurpassed. There are legends and traditions which tell of the strongest educational system in Europe, with sixty universities providing training in science, geometry, mathematics, jurisprudence, philosophy, poetry, oratory, and astronomy. Supposedly, the full offering required twenty years to complete, and many thousands of students attended these universities. Pontius Pilate is said to have gone to Britain to study in the universities of that country. (Ref. 12:54,55)

RELIGIOUS BELIEFS

As will be discussed in Chapters 5 and 6, emigrating Hebrews may have brought their beliefs to Britain before and during the time of Abraham, possibly as early as 2300 B.C. Elements of Hebrew language and tradition have been identified in Wales.

According to this premise, Israelite beliefs and Mosaic patterns of worship were strongly entrenched in early Britain, and Mosaic law governed the people and provided the foundation for later government. Legend has it that when Christ's apostles brought Christianity to Britain, their teachings were readily accepted because the foundation was already there.

Through the ages, Britain has been a bastion for Christianity. When Latter-day Saint prophets brought the restored gospel to Britain in 1837, many of the inhabitants were readily receptive. They had been prepared for and were seeking further light and knowledge.

The prophet of the restoration, Joseph Smith, stated in conference in 1831 that John the Beloved was then ministering among the lost tribes of Israel, preparing them for their return. (Ref. 31:176) Latter-day Apostle Heber C. Kimball, when inquiring of the Prophet about the significance of strong spiritual feelings while laboring in the Preston area of western England, was told that ancient prophets had preceded his labors there. (Ref. 10:193)

CHAPTER THREE

EARLY MIGRATIONS TO THE ISLES OF THE SEA

Legends of early migrations can be preserved in
several ways. Such records of the past may be
found in written accounts including scriptures, or recorded on stone monuments, or preserved in oral legends and
traditions. Any one of these sources may present only a
clouded picture of the past. But clarity and continuity are
much more likely when all available sources can be carefully considered. Hugh Nibley (Ref. 26:510) said "Nothing
is harder than to convince a man of a thing he has not
experienced." Some of the information and ideas to be
presented in this book may be new—the reader's patient
and open-minded consideration will allow the patterns
and significance of the concepts in this book to reveal
themselves more clearly.

PLACE OF ORIGIN

Genesis 8:4 tells us that Noah's ark came to rest upon
the mountains of Ararat, which tradition places on the
frontier of Turkey, Iran, and Armenia. Noah's family dispersed, with most of Japheth's descendants said to have
gone north and northeast into Asia, Ham's family west-

ward into the eastern Mediterranean area and Egypt, and Shem's principally into the Tigris and Euphrates valleys.

Using Bible chronology, Eber, a great-grandson of Noah, was born about 280 years before Noah died. Eber's descendants became known as Hebrews. The name "Eber," or "Heber" means "to cross" in the Hebrew language. Abraham was born about 240 years before Eber died, and—by his pre-covenant name "Abram"—was the first man in history to be specifically identified as a Hebrew (see Genesis 14:13).

Hugh Nibley calls attention to the inference in Genesis 10 regarding the "generations of the sons of Noah" that, when the Tower of Babel was built after the flood, Noah's family had already begun "...moving out in all directions from a common center." (Ref. 26:23, 673)

EARLY BRITONS

Early migrations into Britain are by tradition said to have begun as early as the time of Noah, soon after the flood. Noah's descendants will be referred to hereafter as Hebrews, descendants of Shem and his grandson Eber, but legends indicate that some were also from the line of Japheth.

Jacob, Abraham's grandson, had his name changed to Israel by Jehovah. Thereafter his posterity were known as Israelites. Major Israelite migrations into the Mediterranean area and into Britain could have begun while the main body of Israel was in Egypt. Other groups may have migrated during the 40 years Israel was in the wilderness following the exodus from Egypt. About 100 years after the ten northern tribes of Israel were captured and deported into Assyria, legend says that they fled north and became lost to the knowledge of the world. Many of these Israelite refugees supposedly migrated into western Asia and northern Europe, with many from Ephraim and Judah traditionally believed to have invaded Britain as Celts, Angles, Saxons, Jutes, Danes and Normans.

HEBREWS

Some traditions persist that Hebrews were the first immigrants to the Isles of the Sea, identified in legend with Britain. Referred to as Kelts (or "Celts"), these Hebrews are said to have come to a virgin land devoid of human habitation. (Ref. 16:86)

According to traditions about the religion of these early settlers, we find that the universe was their bible. They established calendars based on observed movements of heavenly bodies; clearly defined times, seasons, days and years; fixed the dates of religious festivals; and regulated agriculture by changing random plantings and harvestings into rhythmic, annual cycles. (Ref. 16:18) Archeological evidence indicates that the people of this period possessed a remarkably clear understanding of the relationships among the heavenly bodies. There are also indications that they did not worship the sun, the moon, or the stars, but that they worshipped the creator of the heavens, giving thanks for the blessings of light and energy conveyed to them by these creations of God.

E. O. Gordon makes a very significant comment regarding these ancient people:

> One of the greatest testimonies to the spiritual character of the religion of our forefathers is the fact that no graven image or inscribed stone of any kind has ever been discovered of Pre-Roman origin in Great Britain. Among the relics of the Stone, Bronze, and Iron Ages in the British Antiquities Department of the British Museum, there is no evidence whatever of idolatrous worship, as we find in the Assyrian, Greek or Roman galleries. (Ref. 16:19)

Stonehenge, a circle of gigantic stone monoliths, about 60 miles southwest of London and eight miles north of Salisbury, remains as one of the earliest structures created by early Britons. (See Figures 2, 3 and 4) Recent studies confirm that the stones comprising Stonehenge were placed in a position to coincide with the rising and setting of heavenly bodies, making the entire monument an astronomical observatory. (Ref. 6:47-52)

Existing Roman records have asserted that human sacrifices occurred at Stonehenge. Archeological excavations have now led scholars to believe that only animal offerings were made, a practice which would be in accordance with Mosaic law. (Ref. 12:65-66)

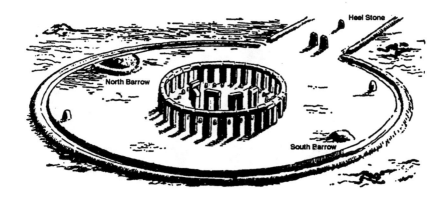

Figure 2
Reconstruction of Stonehenge (Ref. 16:20)

Figure 3
Sunrise at Stonehenge (Ref. 16:57)

Figure 4
Stonehenge Today (Ref. 28:67)

More than 700 sites in Britain contain remnants of stone circles and stone altars. E. Raymond Capt reports (Ref. 6:57) that a Professor Thom measured hundreds of stone monuments all over Britain and found that the standard unit of measurement was 2.72 feet or 32.62 inches, which he called the "Megalithic Yard". "Stonehenge, however, is unique in that the builders used the Egyptian Royal Cubit [20.63 inches] in its construction, and the Megalithic yard elsewhere." Both the Royal Cubit and the Sacred Cubit [25.03 inches] were used in the Great Pyramid of Egypt. (Ref. 8:118-120) These measurements and other archeological data offer strong evidence that both the Pyramids and Stonehenge were constructed very early by God-fearing men having a common cultural origin and a remarkable understanding of astronomy.

"As the result of archeological excavations and investigations, it is now concluded that the building of Stonehenge covered a span of about 900 years: between 2300 and 1400 B.C." (Ref. 6:23) The Great Pyramid in Egypt was constructed about the same time as the initial construction at Stonehenge.

George Jowett states that the British archeologist, Sir William Flinders Petrie, discovered at Old Gaza in the Near East gold ornaments and enamelware of Celtic origin from Britain made about 1500 B.C., and also found Egyptian beads at Stonehenge in England.

Linguistic studies also confirm associations between early Britons and the Near East. Jowett says that "...the Keltic or Cymeric tongue is the oldest living language. Its root words have a basic affinity with ancient Hebrew. ... The ancient language is still alive. It is frequently spoken in Wales, Cornwall, Ireland, Scotland, and in Brittany and Normandy." (Ref. 18:37,38) E. O. Gordon details many similarities in tradition, language, and moral codes between Britain and the Near East. (Ref. 16)

George N. Wilson asks the question "How did we—the British—get our name?" and then queries "...is it not a strange coincidence that in the ancient Hebrew ... BRITH means 'covenant' and ISH means 'man,' so BRIT-ISH means 'covenant man.' AIN means 'land,' so BRITH or BRIT-AIN means 'Land of the Covenant.'" (Ref. 36:8) The Jewish Encyclopedia, Vol. 2, pp. 509 and 567, lists these same definitions for BRIT, BERIT, IAN and ISH.

> Tradition connects many Hebrew names and over 6,000 Hebrew-related words with the Welsh language. Ancient Welsh is believed by some to be nearly pure Hebrew. An account of a very early migration of Kymry (or Cymry) to Britain is recorded in the Welsh Triads. E. O. Gordon quotes from
>
> ...the account of the colonization of the isle of Britain, gathered principally from the Triads and Druidic remains collected by the eminent Welsh scholar and bard Rev. R. W. Morgan (P. C. Tregynon). [sic] ... "[The Kymry] found no living creature on it but bisons, elks, bears, beavers, and water monsters. ... [A]nd they called the Island the White Island (Ynys Wen)." (Ref. 16: 85-86)

Today the Welsh still refer to themselves as the People of Cymri. (Ref. 16:11)

A second major migration to Britain may have occurred five centuries later, after the break-up of the Trojan Empire ca. 1190 B.C., perhaps leading to the settlements that eventually became the London of today. Another early document reporting the origin of London "is to be found in a Latin Chronicle, in which Edward the Confessor speaks of London as...a city founded and built after the likeness of Great Troy." (Ref. 16:90-91)

> The conclusion that can be drawn from all the evidence is that the early Britons who erected Stonehenge and other great megalithic monuments were either Hebrews themselves or progenitors of the Hebrews. They were the "Building Race" of the Bible, fathered by Shem. They built the Great Pyramid in Egypt. Down through the ages, groups of these people were continually moving westward, coming finally into the British Isles. They brought with them the knowledge, ability and acumen that enabled them to build Stonehenge. (Ref. 6:69)

European megalithic sites suggest that the peoples migrating into Britain were following Jehovah's instructions to Ephraim to "Set thee up waymarks, make thee high heaps: set thine heart toward the highway." (Jeremiah 31:21) Capt also comments earlier in his book on the stone structures built and left along migration routes:

> The waymarks of the megalithic builders can be traced by the remains of their monuments (circles and mounds) forming a westward trail, between 3000 and

4000 years old. Beginning in the district north of the Persian Gulf, the route is found both north and south of the Mediterranean Sea to the coasts of Western Europe. From Portugal and the Bay of Biscay in Brittany the trail separates, one going into Denmark, Sweden and Norway. (Ref. 6:59)

These stone structures can be roughly divided into three classes:

1. Menhirs (Celtic—"high stone"): Single upright stones which may be commemorative of some great event or personage.
2. Dolmens (Celtic—"table stone"): A stone slab set table-wise on three or more uprights.
3. Cromlechs (Celtic—"stone circle"): A circle of stones sometimes enclosing barrows (tombs) or dolmens.
Stonehenge is a highly specialized example of this last class. (Ref. 6:59)
Sir Henry Morton, the famous British explorer, describes a circle of stones on the summit of Mt. Gerezim ("the Mount of God"). He terms this the oldest Sanctuary in Palestine, and states it is nearly identical with the so-called Druidic circles of Britain. (Ref. 6:69)

Stone slabs set table-wise on three or more stone uprights have been discovered across Europe and in several locations in the Near East. Some scholars believe that the stone megaliths constructed across Europe were constructed much later than the massive circles in England.

If so, that chronology may further confirm that the

early builders were Hebrews who came across Europe to England about the time of the dispersion following the building of the Tower of Babel. Later, significant numbers of Israelites left the main body, after their departure from Egypt ca. 1486 B.C., and migrated into Europe.

According to tradition, the Ten Tribes of Israel who fled north from Assyria about 600 B.C. moved more slowly across Asia and Europe, some not reaching Britain for several centuries, leaving behind their places of worship built of stone. More data will be presented in Chapter 5 concerning these various migrations.

ISRAELITES

A brief outline of the history of Israel will add clarity to the subsequent discussion of migrations to Britain. The children of Abraham, Isaac, and Jacob (Israel) are shown in Figure 5.

Of Abraham's children, Isaac, whose mother was Sarah, was given the birthright. Abraham's son Ishmael, whose mother was Hagar, an Egyptian handmaid of Sarah, was the father of the Arab peoples.

Isaac's son Jacob, renamed "Israel" by Jehovah, and who was the son of Rebekah, received the birthright in his generation. His twin brother Esau, the first-born, sold his birthright to Jacob. Esau's posterity lived in the land of Edom (which means "red"). A mutual hatred developed between the Edomites and Israel and war was constant.

The Twelve Tribes of Israel are descendants of the

twelve sons of Israel. The Levites were dispersed among the tribes to perform priestly duties. Each of Joseph's two sons, Ephraim and Manasseh, received tribal status, and Ephraim inherited the birthright of Israel.

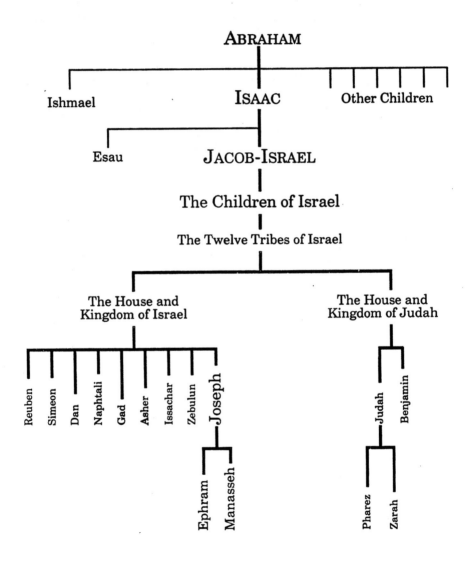

Figure 5
Children of Abraham, Isaac and Jacob-Israel

About 935 B.C., the Tribes of Israel divided into rival kingdoms. The Northern Kingdom, comprising ten tribes under the leadership of Ephraim, was subsequently known as the House and Kingdom of Israel. The Southern Kingdom, consisting of the tribes of Judah and Benjamin, was led by Judah and known as the House and Kingdom of Judah.

Migrations of Judah's descendants occurred under the independent leadership of Judah's twin sons, Pharez and Zarah. The account of their birth, recorded in Genesis 38:27-30, is important because it serves as the basis for distinctive emblems to be discussed in Chapter 4:

> And it came to pass in the time of her travail, that, behold, twins were in her womb. And it came to pass, when she travailed, that the one put out his hand: and the midwife took and bound upon his hand a scarlet thread, saying, This came out first. And it came to pass, as he drew back his hand, that, behold, his brother came out: and she said, How hast thou broken forth? this breach be upon thee: therefore his name was called Pharez. And afterward came out his brother, that had the scarlet thread upon his hand: and his name was called Zarah.

Subsequent discussions of migrations and emblems will distinguish between the descendants of Pharez and the descendants of Zarah.

DISTINCTIVE CHARACTERISTICS OF ISRAELITES

According to the legends and traditions being considered in these chapters, Israelites have migrated to Britain over more than 2500 years. According to Elizabeth Hill Elder, the further we trace the British peoples back through the centuries, the greater becomes their likeness to ancient Israel. Israelite distinctive characteristics are also present in Britain, such as belief in one supreme, living deity; temples; twelve priests; the Mosaic law; language similarities; respect for women; records and chronicles; tribal banners with emblems similar to ancient Israel; battle array similarities; divisions into tens, hundreds and thousands; similar feast days; similar marriage ceremonies; esteem for children; and physical appearance. They were a beautiful people distinctly taller with longer heads than the Mediterranean peoples. (See Ref. 12)

W. H. Fasken believes that the "Roman nose," often thought today to be a distinctive characteristic of Jews, was actually a facial characteristic of Mediterranean peoples who accepted the Jewish faith and became "Jews." According to Fasken, the "Roman nose" was not a characteristic of earlier descendants of Judah. The descendants of Judah were distinctively "long heads" as were the other Israelites. The Mediterranean peoples have been classified by physical anthropologists as "round heads." (Ref. 15:16-22)

MIGRATIONS FOLLOWING THE EXODUS

Considerable evidence, both from history and archae-ology, suggests that a significant number of Israelites may have departed from the main body shortly after the exodus from Egypt about 1486 B.C., and that strong vibrant cultures began to flourish around the Mediterranean Sea and immigrants entered Britain about this time.

Analysis of census figures reported in The Bible, first taken soon after the Israelites left Egypt and taken again 40 years later when they entered Palestine, are indicative that significant numbers left the main body of Israelites during the intervening 40 years. Referring to Table 1, several interesting points are evident.

The total number of men 20 years and older are nearly the same at the beginning and end of the 40 years. However, while Manasseh increased 64 percent, Simeon decreased 63 percent. Benjamin and Asher each increased 29 percent and Issachar 18 percent while Ephraim decreased 20 percent and Naphtali 15 percent. Comparing the larger increases and considering the prob-able increase in family numbers, allowing for the deaths of all who left Egypt, it seems reasonable to expect a probable increase of 30 percent in the whole population.

ISRAEL CENSUS DATA
(MEN 20 YEARS AND OLDER)

Tribe	Exodus from Egypt (Exodus 38:26)	40 years later (Numbers 26:51)	Percent Change
Menasseh	32,300	52,700	+64%
Benjamin	35,400	45,600	+29%
Asher	41,500	53,400	+29%
Issachar	54,400	64,300	+18%
Zebulun	57,400	60,500	+5%
Judah	74,600	76,500	+3%
Dan	62,700	64,400	+3%
Reuben	46,500	43,730	-6%
Gad	45,650	40,500	-11%
Naphtali	53,400	45,400	-15%
Ephraim	40,500	32,500	-20%
Simeon	59,300	22,200	-63%
Total	*603,550*	*601,730*	

Table 1
Israel Census Data

A 30 percent increase means more than 180,000 men age 20 and older. On this basis, Ephraim's decrease of 20 percent means that approximately 20,000 Ephraimite men with their families could have left the main body during the 40 years. If such estimates could be confirmed, they would be indicative that a significant number of Israelites, perhaps 500,000 men, women and children, left the main body of Israel and migrated to other lands during the 40 years following the Exodus from Egypt.

NORTHERN KINGDOM OF ISRAEL DEPORTED TO ASSYRIA

The Northern Kingdom of Israel, consisting of ten of the tribes of Israel, had its capital in Samaria and was led by the tribe of Ephraim.

> In 745 B.C. arose ... the Tiglath Pileser of the Bible (II Kings VX, 29, and XVI, 7 et seq.). He not only directed the transfer of the Israelites to Media (the "Lost Ten Tribes" whose ultimate fate has exercised to many curious minds), but he conquered and ruled Babylon, so founding what historians know as the New Assyrian Empire. His son, Shalmaneser IV (II Kings XVII, 3), died during the siege of Samaria and was succeeded by a usurper, who, no doubt to flatter Babylonian susceptibilities, took the ancient Akkadian Sumerian name of Sargon—Sargon II. He seems to have armed the Assyrian forces for the first time with iron weapons. It was probably Sargon II who actually carried out the deportation of

the Ten Tribes that Tiglath Pileser III had ordered. (Ref. 40:142)

Many historians of this era feel that the Israelites may have been taken to the far northern part of Assyria beyond both the Euphrates and Tigris Rivers, near the western portion of the Caspian Sea (see Figure 6). Subsequent invasions and deportations occurred around 721, 715 and 677 B.C. Assyrians then colonized Samaria, and thus began the intense dislike of the Jews for the imported "Samaritans."

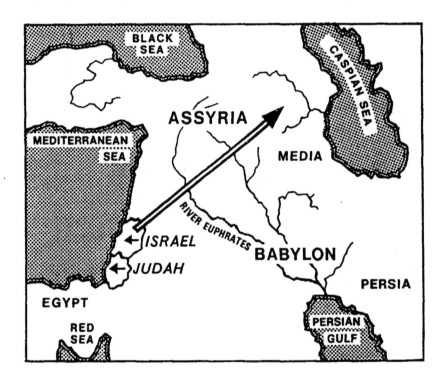

Figure 6
Northern Kingdom of Israel Deported to Assyria (Ref. 4:12)

In 612 B.C., Babylon conquered the Assyrian Empire. The Israelites, the Ten Tribes of Israel who had been deported, took advantage of the break-up of the Assyrian Empire, tradition tells us, and fled to the north out of reach of both Assyrians and Babylonians. The only record of their departure is found in the Apocrypha as quoted below:

> Those are the ten tribes, which were carried away prisoners out of their own land in the time of Osea the king, whom Shalmanezer the king of Assyria led away captive, and he carried them over the waters, and so came they into another land. But they took this counsel among themselves, that they would leave the multitude of the heathen, and go forth into a further country, where never mankind dwelt, that they might there keep their statutes, which they never kept in their own land. And they entered into Euphrates by the narrow passage of the river. For the [M]ost High then shewed signs for them, and held still the flood till they were passed over. For through that country there was a great way to go, namely, of a year and a half: and the same region is called Arsareth. (Apocrypha, 2 Esdras 13:40-41)

The following comment by George Reynolds on the writings of Esdras is helpful:

> They determined to go to a country "where never men dwelt," that they might be free from all contaminating influences. That country could only be found in the north. Southern Asia was already the seat of a comparatively ancient civilization. Egypt flourished in northern Africa,

and southern Europe was rapidly filling with the future rulers of the world. They had, therefore, no choice but to turn their faces northward.

The upper course of the Euphrates lies among lofty mountains and near the village of Pastash, it plunges through a gorge formed by precipices more than a thousand feet in height and so narrow that it is bridged at the top; it shortly afterward enters the plains of Mesopotamia. How accurately this portion of the river answers the description of Esdras of the narrows, where the Israelites crossed.

From the Euphrates the wandering host could take but one course in their journey northward, and that was along the back or eastern shore of the Black Sea. All other roads were impassable to them, as the Caucasian range of Mountains with only two or three passes throughout its whole extent, ran as a lofty barrier from the Black to the Caspian Sea. To go east would take them back to Media, and a westward journey would carry them through Asia Minor to the coasts of the Mediterranean. Skirting along the Black Sea, they would pass the Caucasian range, cross the Kuban River, be prevented by the Sea of Azof from turning westward and would soon reach the present home of the Don Cossaks. (Ref. 29:27-28)

Bruce R. McConkie elaborates on the condition of the Lost Tribes after their departure from Assyria:

The Lost Tribes are not lost unto the Lord. In their northward journeyings they were led by prophets and inspired leaders. They had their Moses and their Lehi, were guided by the spirit of revelation, kept the law of

Moses, and carried with them the statutes and judgments which the Lord had given them in ages past. They were still a distinct people many hundreds of years later, for the resurrected Lord visited and ministered among them following his ministry on this continent among the Nephites (3 Ne. 16:1-4;17:4). Obviously he taught them in the same way and gave them the same truths which he gave his followers in Jerusalem and on the American continent; and obviously they recorded his teachings, thus creating volumes of scripture comparable to the Bible and the Book of Mormon. (Ref. 23:457)

George Reynolds states that a Mr. Ed Hine [reference not noted] wrote that in early Anglo-Saxon times, before coming into Britain, the Saxon's god in human nature "presented himself among these people about the same time as the true Messiah appeared among the Jews. The name of 'the pretender' was Odin or Wodin and he was esteemed the great dispenser of happiness to his followers." (Ref. 29:46-47)

Since the Saxons subsequently "placed his image in the most holy place" in their temple, the question can be asked: was this in truth the promised visit of the resurrected Messiah to the Ten Tribes? Perhaps it is not too much to hope for evidence of Christ's visit to the lost tribes of Israel being revealed soon, now that the restored gospel is being carried to these people.

SOUTHERN KINGDOM OF ISRAEL DEPORTED TO BABYLON

Nebuchadnezzar, King of Babylon, repeatedly invaded the kingdom of Judah, which consisted primarily of the two tribes of Judah and Benjamin. Jerusalem was totally destroyed ca. 581 B.C. and those who survived were deported to the lower Euphrates and Tigris River valleys. (Figure 7)

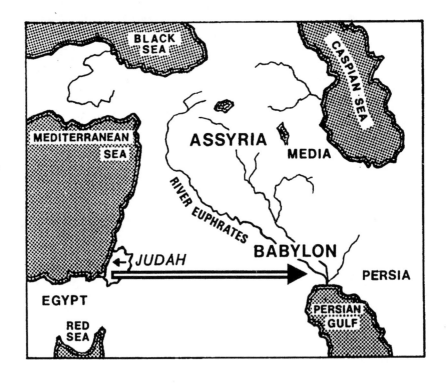

Figure 7
Southern Kingdom of Israel Deported to Babylon (Ref. 4:13)

In 536 B.C. Cyrus the Great of Persia allowed the Jews and their prophets to return to Jerusalem and rebuild their temple (Figure 8), but many of the Jews remained in Babylon. Others were scattered before and during the invasion. Some Jews migrated into the Mediterranean countries and into Europe and Britain from the time of the Exodus until their final scattering when the Romans in 70 A.D. destroyed Jerusalem and the temple again.

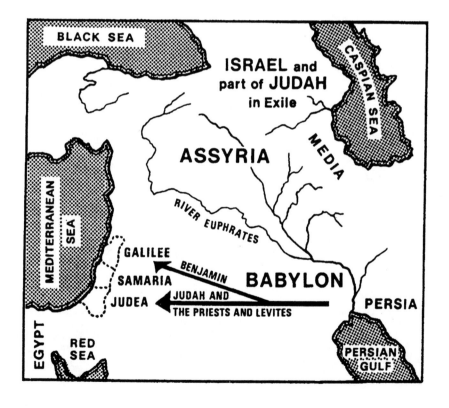

Figure 8
Return of Southern Kingdom (Ref. 4:14)

ISRAEL SCATTERED AND LOST

If the British Isles (presumed by some writers to be the biblical "Isles of the Sea") contain a goodly number of Israelites, the words of prophets recorded in holy scripture can provide a better understanding of what has occurred and what might be expected to occur, for "Surely the Lord God will do nothing, but he revealeth his secret unto his servants the prophets." (Amos 3:7)

About 580 B.C., the American prophet Nephi recorded in The Book of Mormon one of the clearest statements of Israel's scattered and lost condition:

> ...for it appears that the house of Israel, sooner or later, will be scattered upon all the face of the earth, and also among all nations. And behold, there are many who are already lost from the knowledge of those who are at Jerusalem. Yea, the more part of all the tribes have been led away; and they are scattered to and fro upon the isles of the sea; and whither they are none of us knoweth, save that we know that they have been led away. (1 Nephi 22:3-4)

The Book of Mormon itself stands as a witness that the resurrected Savior spent several days on the American continent with a remnant of Israel, the Nephites, whose forebears had fled Jerusalem about 600 B.C. This visit is reported in 3 Nephi, chapters 11 through 27. Latter-day Saints see in it a direct fulfillment of the prophecy made by the Savior and reported by John that "other sheep I have, which are not of this fold: them also I must bring, and they shall hear my voice; and there shall be one fold, and one shepherd." (John 10:16)

Before Christ departed from the Nephites, he made the following statement. "But now I go unto the Father, and also to show myself unto the lost tribes of Israel, for they are not lost unto the Father, for he knoweth whither he hath taken them." (3 Nephi 17:4)

Today, we have the record of his teachings to the Jews—The New Testament—and the record of his teachings to a branch of Israel in America—The Book of Mormon. We can look forward to the record of his teachings to the lost tribes of Israel.

> For behold, I shall speak unto the Jews and they shall write it; and I shall also speak unto the Nephites and they shall write it; and I shall also speak unto the other tribes of the house of Israel, which I have led away, and they shall write it; and I shall also speak unto all nations of the earth and they shall write it. And it shall come to pass that the Jews shall have the words of the Nephites, and the Nephites shall have the words of the Jews; and the Nephites and the Jews shall have the words of the lost tribes of Israel; and the lost tribes of Israel shall have the words of the Nephites and the Jews. (2 Nephi 29:12-13)

Related predictions of the scattering of Israel are recorded in The Bible:

> For the Lord shall smite Israel, as a reed is shaken in the water, and he shall root up Israel out of this good

land, which he gave to their fathers, and shall scatter
them beyond the river. (1 Kings 14:15)

And the Lord shall scatter you among the nations,
and ye shall be left few in number among the heathen,
whither the Lord shall lead you. (Deuteronomy 4:27)

I will sift the house of Israel among all nations.
(Amos 9:9)

Jehovah's Concern for Israel

The Lord took the people of Israel from the land of
their fathers and placed them by great waters, and the
tree of their lineage flourished, as recorded by Ezekiel.
Legend tells us that this tree also flourished in Britain
and in her colonies, and scripture supports the implica-
tion that this kind of colonization took place:

> He took also of the seed of the land, and planted it in
> a fruitful field; he placed it by great waters, and set it as
> a willow tree. And it grew, and became a spreading vine
> of low stature, whose branches turned toward him, and
> the roots thereof were under him: so it became a vine,
> and brought forth branches, and shot forth sprigs.
> (Ezekiel 17:5,6)
>
> Joseph is a fruitful bough, even a fruitful bough by a
> well; whose branches run over the wall. (Genesis 49:22)

After Israel divided into two kingdoms, Judah became
known as the high tree and the green tree, having dili-
gently kept the commandments. (The general interpreta-
tion is that the Northern Kingdom of Israel was the low

tree.) After Judah's downfall, in 581 B.C., Ezekiel wrote:

> And all the trees of the fields shall know that I the
> Lord have brought down the high tree, have exalted the
> low tree, have dried up the green tree, and have made the
> dry tree to flourish. (Ezekiel 17:24)

The Lord spoke to Jeremiah at the time of Judah's pending capture and directed him as follows: "Go and proclaim these words toward the north, and say, return, thou backsliding Israel, saith the Lord." (Jeremiah 3:12) Legends and early commentaries suggest, as will be discussed in Chapter 5, that Jeremiah emigrated to scattered Israel in the British Isles and greatly impacted its future. It is the premise of this book that the nation of Great Britain and its colonies, including America, has for centuries been a light unto the Gentiles.

MIGRATIONS OF ISRAEL

Migrations of lost Israel from their homeland to Assyria, then through Asia, Europe, and into the British Isles, have long been studied. Written records, legends, archeology and paleontology have yielded fragments of information which, when compiled, form a reasonably coherent picture. E. Raymond Capt has summarized Israel's routes of travel and their identities and dates. (Ref. 6:85-88) These are shown in Figure 9.

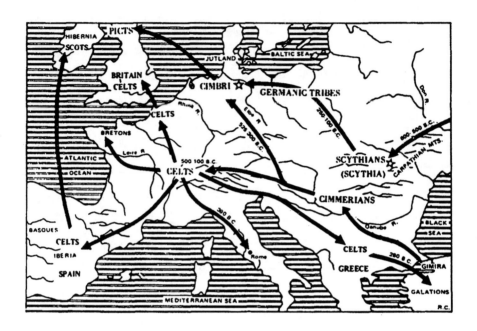

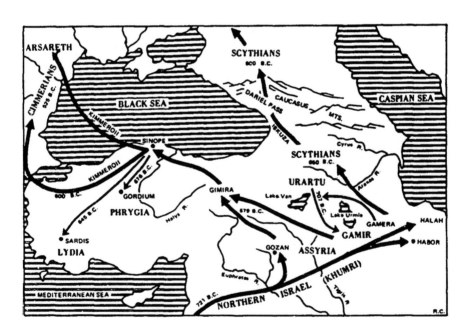

Figure 9
Migrations of Israel (Ref. 6:85-88)

L. G. A. Roberts (Ref. 33) has shown migrations to Britain occurring across the Mediterranean, Asia and Europe. (See Figure 10) Roberts' work updates an old map of Cellarius, 1703 A.D., and also includes information lately found in the earlier writings of Herodotus and others. Traditionally, migrations of Israelites from the Near East to Europe and Britain occurred about 1600 B.C. Final migrations of Normans (also believed to be descended from the Israelites) occurred in 1066 A.D. at the time of William the Conqueror. Thus migrations of Israelites to Britain have presumably covered a span of more than 2,500 years.

Figure 10
Migrations of Israel into Britain after Roberts (Ref. 33)

Archibald F. Bennett details much evidence from archaeology, history and genealogy of the migration of Israel into western Russia, Europe and Britain, Scandinavia and Holland. (Ref. 3:67, etc.) Included are epitaphs in Hebrew from tombs excavated by the Russian Archaeological Society. Specifically mentioned on these epitaphs are the tribes of Naphtali, Simeon, Reuben, Manasseh, and Levi.

> From the identical region where the Ten Tribes were lost in captivity are traced tribes whose descendants spread over Europe. Herodotus, the earliest Greek historian, about 450 B.C., minutely described an ancient group of nomads who he called "Scythians" which then inhabited Crimea and the South Russian steppe from the Don to the Dniester. Before them, in this same area, had formerly dwelt the "Cimmerians."
>
> As they increased they divided into tribes and spread in conquering waves of migration over Europe, mixing "among the people." The mounds of the Black Sea region, of Scandinavia, and of elsewhere in Europe are the waymarks and high heaps of Ephraim. (Ref 3: 73,76)

Identities of specific tribes of Israel seem to have been retained, for instance, the tribe of Dan through such names as Danmar, Denmark, Danube and numerous other place names across central Europe. Fasken states "...that it was Israel, and principally the tribe of Dan, which furnished the human element of classic Greece." (Ref. 15:64)

Darda (1 Kings 4:31), grandson of Judah, called

Dardanu by Josephus, left his identity on the land. Legend tells us that he gave the name Dardania to part of western Asia Minor and that his grandson Tros built the famous city of Troy. The Dardanelles yet stand. James Anderson claims that "Dardanus was ancestor of the Trojan line of kings." (Ref. 1:19,20) Following the defeat of Troy, many of the refugees are believed to have joined the general migration of Israel north and west.

According to George N. Wilson, the Scottish Declaration of Independence, dated 1320 A.D., asserts "...that they [the Scots] 'came from Greater Scythia, passing through the Pillars of Hercules [Gibraltar], sojourned a while in Spain, and thence [proceeded] to settle in Scotland,' one thousand two hundred years after the outgoing of the People of Israel from Egypt [which was ca. 286 B.C.]." (Ref. 36:15)

Following the conquest of Palestine by Joshua, the tribe of Asher was assigned land in Upper Galilee. The Phoenicians lived along the Mediterranean coast adjacent to the tribe of Asher. The sea-faring Phoenicians (and possibly the Asherites) may have provided the transportation for Israelite colonists to Spain and Britain.

Legends persist that Phoenician ships carried Cornish tin from the English mines, which was used in Solomon's temple (about 1000 B.C.). Paul R. Cheesman, in The World of the Book of Mormon (1984, pp. 135-142) presents twelve archeological findings inferring early Phoenician presence in the Western Hemisphere. Samuel D. Marble in Before Columbus (1980, pp. 31, 115, 138) indicates Phoenicians crossed the Atlantic as early as 1447 B.C.,

and about 500 B.C., 30,000 Phoenicians sailed past
Gibraltar for the West. Legends and inscriptions further
imply this presence. Phoenicians also may have provided
the ships that carried the Mulekites to America about 586
B.C. (See The Book of Mormon for references to Mulek,
the only surviving son of Zedekiah, last King of Judah,
taken into captivity by the Babylonians.)

A statement by James E. Talmage is pertinent to this
chapter:

> ...Israelites have been so completely dispersed among
> the nations as to give to this scattered people a place of
> importance as a factor in the rise and development of
> almost every large division of the human family. (Ref.
> 34:316)

For, through Abraham's seed "shall all the nations of
the earth be blessed." (Genesis 22:18)

CHAPTER FOUR

ISRAEL'S EMBLEMS

Each of the tribes of ancient Israel appears to have had a distinctive emblem. W. H. Bennett has spent many years identifying these, and drawing modern parallels among national emblems in the British Isles, Scandinavia, Netherlands, other countries in Europe, Canada, and the United States. Identifying the emblems will help to trace specific tribes and enhance our appreciation and recognition of Israel's past and present leadership.

Ephraim's emblem, for example, may be seen in the temples of the Church of Jesus Christ of Latter-day Saints. Oxen bearing a baptismal font is believed to be one of the emblems of Ephraim.

An official booklet issued by the United States Government entitled Our Flag says: "Heraldry is as old as the human race, and the carrying of banners has been the habit of nations since the beginning of time." Each tribe of Israel had a primary emblem (a banner) and one or more secondary emblems to remind them of their unique patriarchal blessing received from Father Jacob (Israel). Jacob called his sons together a short time before he died, and gave to each a blessing. His words are recorded in Genesis 49 and his charge is in verses 1 and 2:

> And Jacob called unto his sons, and said, Gather
> yourselves together, that I may tell you that which shall
> befall you in the last days. Gather yourselves together,
> and hear, ye sons of Jacob; and hearken unto Israel your
> father.

Moses' blessing recorded in Deuteronomy 33 implies a basis for the unique emblems adopted by each tribe. Tribal emblems appear to have evolved from these blessings; the emblems themselves are listed in Table 2 and shown in Figures 11 through 23.

Before considering each emblem, let's look at a brief discussion of Israel's camp and leadership during the 40 years in the wilderness after leaving Egypt. This will clarify the initial use of these emblems or tribal standards (flags).

Israel's Encampment

The second chapter in the Book of Numbers tells us that Jehovah had directed the twelve tribes to camp around the tabernacle in specific areas. This configuration is shown in Figure 11. Four brigade leaders were appointed: Judah, Reuben, Ephraim, and Dan. Both tribal and brigade standards were adopted. The tribal flags with their unique emblems were displayed when camped around the tabernacle and when moving to a new location. "Every man of the children of Israel shall pitch by his own standard, with the ensign of their father's house...." (Numbers 2:2)

ISRAEL'S TRIBAL EMBLEMS

W. H. Bennett (Ref. 4) in his Symbols of our Celto-Saxon Heritage has presented not only the symbols of each tribe but also the use of these tribal symbols in the emblems of 12 modern countries. His monumental work portrays in a very graphic manner the extent to which emblems of ancient Israel have survived in countries, provinces and cities of Europe. The discussions and illustrations of Israel's emblems in this chapter are based upon Bennett's excellent publication. Bennett acknowledges with appreciation the contribution of many sources to his understanding of Israelite emblems in their respective heraldry. (Ref. 4:xiii)

Bennett's extensive efforts to gather heraldic evidence continued over 30 years, yet he states that what he has presented is only a part of what is available. L. G. Pine, commenting upon Bennett's work, states that "the mass of testimony adduced by Mr. Bennett is too strong to be ignored." (Ref. 4:xvii)

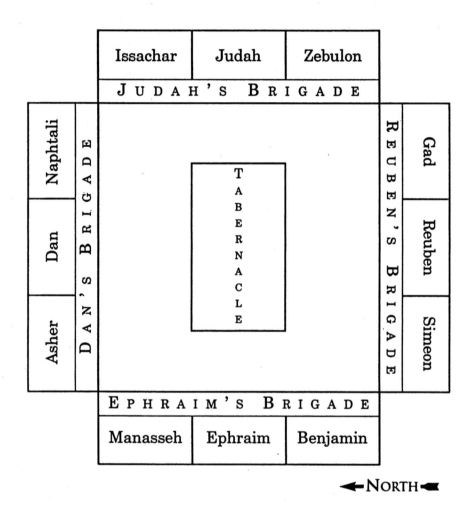

Figure 11
Israel's Encampment Around the Tabernacle
(Each tribe had its standard; each three-tribe brigade had its
standard)

EMBLEMS OF ISRAEL

TWELVE TRIBES	PRIMARY EMBLEMS	SECONDARY EMBLEMS
Judah	Lion	Three Lions
Ephraim	Ox	Unicorn and Horn
Manasseh	Olive Branch	Bundle of Arrows
Dan	Serpent	Horse
Reuben	Man	Body of Water
Simeon	Sword	Castle Gate
Zebulun	Ship	
Asher	Covered Goblet	
Benjamin	Wolf	
Naphtali	Hind or Stag	
Gad	Leader on Horse	
Issachar	Ass under a burden	

BRIGADES	BRIGADE EMBLEMS
Judah	Lion
Ephraim	Ox
Dan	Eagle
Reuben	Man

OTHER EMBLEMS:
• Quartered Shield
• Shield of David
• Harp of David
• Breastplate of the High Priest

EMBLEMS OF ZARAH-JUDAH WERE:
• Red Hand and Cord and,
• Rampant Red Lion

EMBLEMS OF THE TWO KINGDEMS OF ISRAEL WERE:
• Crowned Lion of the Kingdem of Judah (Southern Kingdom) and,
• Unicorn of the Kingdem of Israel (Northern Kingdom)

Table 2
Emblems of Israel

Figure 12
Emblems of the Tribe of Judah (Ref. 4:25)

Figure 13
Emblems of the Tribe of Ephraim (Ref. 4:30, 31)

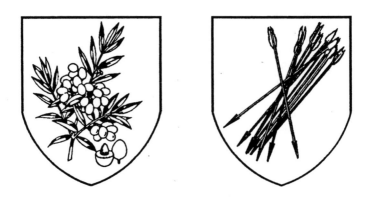

Figure 14
Emblems of the Tribe of Manasseh (Ref. 4:29)

Figure 15
Emblems of the Tribe of Dan (Ref. 4:26

Figure 16
Emblems of the Tribe of Reuben (Ref. 4:23)

Figure 17
Emblems of the Tribe of Simeon (Ref. 4:24)

Figure 18
Emblem of the Tribe of Zebulun (Ref. 4:29)

Figure 19
Emblem of the Tribe of Asher (Ref. 4:28)

Figure 20
Emblem of the Tribe of Benjamin (Ref. 4:31)

Figure 21
Emblem of the Tribe of Naphtali (Ref. 4:27)

Figure 22
Emblem of the Tribe of Gad (Ref. 4:27)

Figure 23
Emblem of the Tribe of Issachar (Ref. 4:28)

QUARTERED SHIELD

When Israel was camped in the wilderness, three tribes were on each side of the tabernacle, forming four brigades, as shown in Figure 11 above. The cross which often appears on the shields of heraldry dividing the shield into four quadrants may be a direct descendant of the four brigades of Israel.

FOUR BRIGADE EMBLEMS

The four brigade emblems are shown in Figure 24. Judah is represented by the Lion, Reuben by the Man, Ephraim by the Ox, and Dan by the Eagle. Relatively few emblems of other tribes are used in national heraldry, because they were usually identified by the emblem of the brigade to which they belonged. Thus Benjamin, as a member of the Southern Kingdom of Judah, would frequently be identified by the Lion, the emblem of the Brigade of Judah. The more frequent use of brigade emblems does not necessarily indicate that the other tribes of the brigade were not in the country. Heraldry related to provinces and municipalities usually includes more emblems of individual tribes than does national heraldry.

Two visions, one seen by Ezekiel and the other by John the Revelator, each mention the four brigade emblems, adding credibility to them. Ezekiel 1:5-10 records four living creatures, each having the faces of a man, a lion, an ox and an eagle. John, in Revelations 4:7, also records four beasts, like a lion, a calf, a man and an eagle.

OTHER EMBLEMS

Descendants of Judah used several other emblems. They are the Shield of David, the Harp of David, the Breastplate of the High Priest, and the emblems of Zarah-Judah. The two kingdoms of Israel also used distinctive emblems.

Figure 24
Brigade Emblems (Ref. 4:64)

SHIELD OF DAVID

The six-pointed star (Figure 25) known as the Shield or Star of David is used extensively. The shield consists of two overlapping and entwined equilateral triangles. One triangle points upward, symbolic of man's supplications to heaven; the other triangle points downward, symbolic of God's blessings to man.

Figure 25
Shield or Star of David (Ref. 4:102)

In addition to the extensive use of the Shield of David in European heraldry, it is centered in the flag of the State of Israel. The Ethiopian Royal Standard incorporated a crowned Lion of Judah. On Temple Square in Salt Lake City, a beautiful stained glass window in the Assembly Hall portrays the Shield of David. Many provinces and municipal standards contain the Shield of David. The Shield of David is used extensively in the United States as an emblem within the badge used by law enforcement agencies.

HARP OF DAVID

King David was not only a great leader, but also a poet and a musician as attested in the Psalms. The Harp of David (Figure 26) is often used in heraldry to convey the ancestral tie of royalty to David.

Figure 26
Harp of David (Ref. 4: 99)

BREASTPLATE OF THE HIGH PRIEST

The high priest, at the time of Moses, wore a breast-plate as part of his sacred attire. (Figure 27) This was called the "breastplate of judgment." (Exodus 28:13-30; 39:8-21) It contained twelve precious stones, arranged in three columns of four stones each, symbolic of the twelve tribes.

Figure 27
Breastplate of the High Priest (Ref. 4: 126)

EMBLEMS OF ZARAH-JUDAH

Zarah's unique emblems, Figure 28, relate to his birth as one of the twin sons of Judah, recorded in Genesis 38:27-30. At Zarah's birth, the midwife tied a red cord around the wrist of his hand, which protruded first. The hand then withdrew, and Zarah's twin brother Pharez was born first. Then Zarah was delivered. A hand, red from the blood of birth, circled by a scarlet thread or cord, became the distinctive emblem of the Zarah branch of the tribe of Judah. Zarah's lineage is also portrayed by red lions.

Figure 28
Red Emblems of Zarah-Judah (Ref. 4:112-113)

EMBLEMS OF THE TWO KINGDOMS OF ISRAEL

Following the division of Israel into two kingdoms (ca. 922 B.C.), unique but related emblems were needed. The traditional lion of Judah was given a crown as the emblem of the Southern Kingdom of Judah. The unicorn, a horse with a horn, was used as the emblem of the Northern Kingdom of Israel, led by Ephraim (Figure 29). Scriptural basis for selection of the unicorn as the emblem may be in Numbers 23:22 and 24:8 where "the strength of an unicorn" is cited.

Figure 29
Emblems of the Two Kingdoms of Israel (Ref. 4:87)

SURVIVING EXAMPLES OF ISRAEL'S EMBLEMS

Traditionally, the scattering of Israel was to all nations, but primarily and initially into western Asia and Europe along the routes of migration. Colonization in the past 400 years has further dispersed Israel.

> Most of these emblems of Israel are in the countries bordering the North Sea, where they constitute the major element in the populations of Norway, Sweden, Denmark, Iceland and the Netherlands, and probably in Belgium, Luxembourg, Finland and the Ukraine. In smaller proportions they are also to be found in Latvia, Lithuania, Estonia, Switzerland, the Provinces of Normandy and Brittany in France and in some parts of Greece, Romania, Italy, Spain and Germany. (Ref. 4:145)
>
> Further, in the case of Britain and the United States, we have no others! For, with the single exception of the Welsh dragon (which was not the emblem of the ancient Britons), every national emblem of Britain and the United States is an Israel emblem. (Ref. 4:6)

BRITISH ROYAL ARMS

Emblems of heraldry in the British Royal Arms (Figure 30) strongly suggest that leaders of both the Northern Kingdom of Israel and the Southern Kingdom of Judah came to Britain. The state shield is supported by the Crowned Lion of Judah and the Unicorn of Ephraim. One is reminded of Isaiah's prophecy (11:13) that in the last days "Ephraim shall not envy Judah, and Judah shall not vex Ephraim."

On the British Royal Arms are three other symbols of the tribe of Judah; the Three Lions couchant of Pharez-Judah, the Red Lion rampant of Zarah-Judah, and the Harp of David. Also, the shield is quartered, symbolic of the four brigades of Israel. The crowned lion and emblems of Judah within the shield imply that Britain is peopled by descendants of the tribe of Judah. Bible prophecies certainly raise the probability that British rulers are descendants of the House of Israel. 2 Samuel 7:16 records the prophecy of Nathan to King David in which an everlasting covenant was made, guaranteeing that the Royal House would continue to reign: "And thine house and thy kingdom shall be established for ever before thee: thy throne shall be established for ever...." We are also reminded of Jacob's statement in his blessing of Judah (Genesis 49:10): "The scepter shall not depart from Judah...." The British royal scepter is another emblem retained from ancient times.

Figure 30
British Royal Arms (Ref. 4:96)
(from the Silver Jubilee edition of The Queen, 1 May 1935)

As evidenced by their treatment of the Savior during
His life on earth, the ruling Jews in Jerusalem no longer
retained divine authority. In Chapter 5, we will discuss
the tradition that the prophet Jeremiah, from the lineage
of Pharez-Judah, brought his authority to Ireland when
he migrated there. The earlier migration to Ireland of

descendants of the Zarah branch of Judah was presented in Chapter 3. The work of some genealogists has connected these two branches of Judah, describing how the royal leadership of Britain today is descended from both branches of the tribe of Judah (as portrayed on the shield of the British Royal Arms) through the Kings of Ulster and Scotland.

Emblems of the tribe of Judah are used in Britain in several other royal items. The Royal Standard of the British Sovereign has the same three emblems of Judah (the three lions couchant, the red lion rampant, and the harp) as well as the quartered Shield of Israel. On the hilt of the swords of commissioned officers appears the Star of David. Bennett states that "Thus, at least as far back as a thousand years ago the Shield of David was in use in Britain, and long before that in Ulster [Ireland], as an heraldic emblem by the ancestors of our Royal House." (Ref. 4:109)

BRITISH CROWN

The Crown of St. Edward (Figure 31), used in the coronation of British sovereigns, contains twelve jeweled emblems symbolic of the twelve jewels in the breastplate of Israel's high priest (which symbolized the twelve tribes of Israel). The twelve jewels are set around the base of the crown. Just as the Twelve Tribes are in four groups (brigades) of three tribes each, so also the twelve jeweled emblems on the base of the crown are in four groups of three, each marked off by four upright bars.

Figure 31
The Crown of St. Edward (Ref. 4:195)

On the four uprights are four larger stones, symbolic of the four brigade leaders of the Camp of Israel. At the juncture of the uprights rests a jeweled orb and cross, symbolic of God's presence over the world and the twelve tribes of Israel.

Zarah-Judah Emblems in Britain

Early British national emblems contained the emblem of Zarah-Judah, which was the red lion. Later when the Saxons and Normans became rulers of Britain, the dominant emblem became the lion of Pharez-Judah shown earlier in Figure 12.

Scottish Royal Arms (Figure 32) show two unicorns of the Northern Kingdom supporting the shield containing the red lion of Zarah.

Arms of Northern Ireland (Figure 33) show the red lion of Zarah, and a reindeer as supporters of the shield, and two standards containing four distinctive emblems of Israel: the Red Hand of Zarah, the Shield or Star of David, the Harp of David and the Quartered Shield.

Israel's Emblems in the United States

The Great Seal of the United States (Figure 34) contains five emblems of Israel. The eagle is the brigade emblem of Dan. The olive branch is the primary emblem and the bundle of arrows the secondary emblem of

Manasseh. The thirteen stars are arranged to represent the Shield of David and the surrounding circle of clouds is symbolic of the protecting cloud over the Camp of Israel during the exodus.

These same elements are used in the President's Seal and in the President's Colors.

Figure 32
Scottish Royal Arms (Ref. 4: 121)

Figure 33
The Arms of Northern Ireland (Ref. 4:119)

Figure 34
The Great Seal of the United States of America (Ref. 4:140)

ISRAEL'S EMBLEM IN CANADA

Although rotated 90 degrees, the Breastplate of the High Priest of Israel with its supporting chains may be illustrated in the central portion of the Canadian Customs Service cap badge. (Figure 35).

Figure 35
Canadian Customs Service Cap Badge (Ref. 4:134)

Israel in Europe

As discussed in Chapter 3 and shown in Figures 9 and 10, Israel is believed to have migrated in various groups and at various times from the eastern Mediterranean area through Europe to the Isles of the Sea, which are traditionally identified as the British Isles. During these migrations, significant numbers remained in the areas through which they traveled. In time British royalty intermarried with royalty in Europe, passing on to them the emblem of Judah—the lion and other emblems of Israel. Bennett (Ref. 4) details Israel's emblems in the heraldry of the Netherlands, Iceland, Norway, Sweden, Denmark, Belgium, Luxembourg, and Spain.

Conclusions

Bennett's thirty years of study, devoted to identifying Israel's emblems, suggests that the scattered tribes of Israel have migrated to and colonized both Europe and America. Information from eastern Europe and western Asia was not available when Bennett compiled his heraldry research and published it in 1976. Certainly it is possible that a significant portion of the Lost Tribes will be found in these countries.

Chapter 6 will discuss the premise that the gathering of Ephraim has been most fruitful from those countries which show Ephraim's emblems in their national, provincial and municipal heraldry.

CHAPTER FIVE

INDIVIDUALS WITH AN IMPACT

There are many legends of individuals who had a marked impact on early British history, legends that connect Britain to Hebrew and Israelite influence. These individuals came to Britain both by land and by sea. The earliest, supposedly, were Hebrews who built Stonehenge and the gigantic Avebury before the time of Abraham. These early immigrants are thought to have been descendants of Shem and Eber, but none are known by name.

HU GADARN HYSICION

According to some researchers, about 1800 B.C., the legendary Hu the Mighty led the first colony of Cymri from where Constantinople now stands into Britain. This migration is believed to have occurred about the time Jacob and his sons went to Egypt. The name "Hysicion" is said to be a form of Isaacson ("son of Isaac"). Hu is accepted by some as the originator of the early historical records known as the Welsh Triads (Ref. 6:75). "Hu Gadarn was regarded as the personification of intelligence and culture. As a peace maker he stands paramount." (Ref. 16:28,29) Elder makes a significant statement that links Hu to the tribe of Ephraim: "On Hu Gadarn's standard was depicted the Ox," the emblem of Ephraim. (Ref. 12:53)

Hu is traditionally thought to be the father of Druidism. It is interesting to note that Isabel Hill Elder (Ref. 12:71) quotes seven authoritative sources stating that the Latin equivalent for Druids is "Magi." Did the Magi come from Britain searching for the Christ Child? Aspects of Druidism suggest that they were anticipating the birth of a Messiah.

BRUTUS THE TROJAN

Some archaeologists and historians connect the Hebraic culture with the ancient city of Troy. When Troy fell in 1185 B.C., legends tell us, Brutus the Trojan led survivors to Britain and founded a colony on the shores of the Thames River.

This was supposedly about the time of the prophet Samuel. Brutus named his city Caer Troia, better known as Troynovant ("New Troy"). Eventually, the city became known as London (Ref. 16:83, 91, 92, 95, 96). The founders of London were Kymry (Cymri), kinsmen of the earlier settlers brought into Wales by the legendary Hu Gadarn Hysicion.

Gordon states that "The 'Island of Brutus' was the common name of the island of old times," and that the name "Britain" is derived from "Brutus Land." "Brutus' name heads the roll of all the genealogies of the British kings, preserved as faithfully as were those of the kings of

Israel and Judah." (Ref. 16:92) Modern scholars recognize
that identifying Brutus as the founder of London requires
them to accept his legendary genealogy as a descendant
of the Roman (pagan) goddess Venus (through his grandfather Aeneas), a descent which is not, of course, accepted
as historical fact. The point being made here, however, is
that, just as the legends of King Arthur and Homer's
epics of Troy have been proven to have elements of fact
about them, the case of Brutus may prove similar, and a
real, historical personage, yet unknown, eventually be
discovered among the ambiguous and fragmented legendary remains.

The Welsh Triads state that Brutus brought Trojan
law to Britain which he incorporated into the patriarchal
order brought by Hu.

In the epic, Brutus established the Kingdom of
Britain, and put in force many laws concerning human
liberties. He introduced the chariot system of warfare,
and a system for laying out military camps superior to
the Roman system. According to the Triads, Brutus died
after a memorable reign of 24 years. (Ref. 16:96-98)

Prophet Jeremiah

The Bible contains prophecies of Jeremiah over a period of 40 years. He faced continuous opposition and insults
from the priests, the people, the army and the king of
Judah. After Jerusalem was destroyed ca. 581 B.C., the
Bible indicates that he and his faithful scribe Baruch

went to Egypt.

Jeremiah is reported (by several authors who quote from various ancient sources) to have taken Tamar and Scota, daughters of the Jewish King Zedekiah, with him to Egypt. Anthony W. Ivins describes Jeremiah's departure from Jerusalem in this way:

> Zedekiah, at the time, had two daughters. The Prophet Jeremiah was the great-grandfather of these two girls.[1] ... These two beautiful girls were protected against the Babylonians by being placed in the cave of Jeremiah, the prophet. He became their guardian, the custodian of their welfare. ... Jeremiah took them down into Egypt, it is said, to the same place where Joseph and Mary went with Christ, our Lord, at the time of the execution of the decree of Herod by which the children of Bethlehem were put to death. They abode there, at a place called Taphanes, the ruins of which are now well known. The natives refer to it to this day as the palace of the Jew's daughter, or the house of the old Prophet. (See Jeremiah 41:10-12, 14-15 and 43:1-7)
>
> After the conquest of Palestine, the Babylonian armies invaded Egypt and it became evident that they would be victorious over the Egyptians. Just at this time we lose sight of Jeremiah and these two girls, so far as the Bible is concerned.
>
> Just at that time a ship landed upon the coast of Spain, from which an old man and his secretary and two young women disembarked. They remained for a short period in that country, where one of the girls married into

---

[1] It is doubtful that the Prophet Jeremiah was the great-grandfather as Ivins and others have claimed. The great-grandfather of the two daughters of King Zedekiah was Jeremiah of Libnah whose daughter Hamutal married King Josiah the father of King Zedekiah (2 Kings 23:31; 24:15), whereas the Prophet Jeremiah was a son of Hilkiah of the priests that were in Anathoth (Jeremiah 1:1).

the reigning house of Spain, but the old man, who is referred to in Ireland as Ollamh Fodhla (the old prophet), in their traditions and the songs which they still sing of him, passed across the channel and landed on the coast of Ireland, taking with him the elder of the two girls, whose name was Tamar Tephi, which translated from Hebrew to English means the Beautiful Palm, or the Beautiful Wanderer. (Ref. 17:6-8)

According to this legend, the prophet Jeremiah, the princess Tamar Tephi, and the faithful scribe Simon Baruch arrived in Ireland after 581 B.C. Tamar Tephi's grace and beauty were also legendary. She would have been about nineteen years old at this time.

Tea [Tamar] Tephi's marriage to Heremon, King of Eri [Ireland] ... combined for the first time in four hundred years the royal houses of the divided kingdom of Israel. ... Irish pedigrees of the time show them to be descended from the tribes of the Northern Kingdom [of Israel]. (Ref. 38:131; for "Eri" see fn. ref. in 25:8)

Later, King Heremon became the king of the southern part of Scotland by conquest.

[M]odern genealogists now at work upon the collection and definite establishment of genealogical records, trace both the Tudor and the Stuart lines of [British] kings ... directly back to the girl, Tamar Tephi. So it would seem that, unknown to men at the time, the Lord preserved that lineage. ... He has been watching over those people, ... He has been directing them, ... He has been helping them, ... it is He and not their numerical strength that has made Great Britain, Scandinavia, and Germany the dominant powers of the world. (Ref. 17:7,8)

When Jeremiah's party arrived in Ireland,

...they had in their possession, according to Irish history, the great Mergech, the law which was contained in a huge chest. ... Some writers have speculated that the chest contained the Ark of the Covenant. Jeremiah gave to the people new laws which were similar to the Ten Commandments. He is revered as the great law giver. Olam Fodhla [Jeremiah] established a school of the prophets. (Ref. 38: 127, 129)

It is significant that in the historic Four Courts of Dublin there are two important medallion portraits, one of Moses and the other of the great Irish legislator. Moses gave the Law to Israel at Sinai and Jeremiah reinstituted it in the "height of Israel" in Ireland. These remarkable portraits accompany a copy of the ancient laws instituted in Eri. The portrait of Jeremiah is identified by Mr. Glover, an authority upon Irish genealogies and history, as Jeremiah. The Irish have honored him for 2500 years. ... A spot on Devenish Island, the "Holy Isle," in lower Lough Erne, two miles from Enniskillen, is marked as the burial place of the great legislator. (Ref. 38: 129-130)

Jeremiah also brought with him what is called "Jacob's Stone," referred to in Genesis 28:18 as the pillow Jacob had during his dream at Bethel when the Lord blessed him. Jacob took the stone to Egypt and the Israelites carried it with them during the Exodus.

Tradition tells us that it came to Ireland from Bethel and Egypt, thence to Scotland, and today, known as the "Stone of Scone," it rests under the seat of Great Britain's Royal Coronation Chair in Westminster Abbey in London (Figure 36). Tradition reports that every legendary king or queen who reigned on the British throne since the days of Jeremiah was crowned while seated in this chair, as also the documented kings and queens have been, except for "Bloody Mary," who sat in a chair blessed by the Roman Pope.

Queen Tamar Tephi is said to be buried in the Hill of Tara on an isle in Loch Erne, Ireland, in a repository sixty feet square which has never been disturbed since her interment. The large mysterious chest that Jeremiah brought from the Holy Land is said to buried with the Queen. (Ref. 38: 131-132)

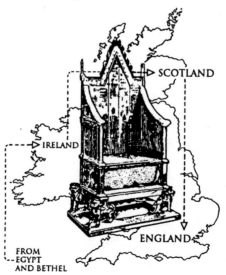

Figure 36
Jacob's Stone under the Seat of the Coronation Chair,
Westminster Abbey (Ref. 4: 95)

JOSEPH OF ARIMATHAEA

Recorded history provides a starting point for considering the possible impact of Joseph of Arimathaea on Britain. The Bible identifies Joseph as a rich man who lived in Arimathaea near Jerusalem. Mark 16:43 states that he was an "honourable counselor," and Luke 14:8 states that he was an "honourable man." John 19:38 refers to him as "a disciple of Jesus," and Luke 23:50 says he was "a good man, and a just." Luke 23:51 further states that he "had not consented to the counsel and deed of them," referring to the action of the Sanhedrin condemning Christ. Joseph was a member of the Sanhedrin. He was a Senator, and had the Roman title of "Nobilis Decurio." This title indicates that he held a prominent position in the Roman administration as a minister of mines. He was a wealthy Jew with considerable influence in Roman as well as Jewish circles. (Ref. 18:17)

TIN TRADE

Joseph's wealth reputedly came from tin, which came from Cornwall in England. The eminent British historian, Sir Edward Creasy, writes in his History of England: "The British mines supplied the glorious adornment of Solomon's Temple." (Ref. 18:42)

Historians Herodotus (as early as 445 B.C.), Pytheas (352-323 B.C.), and Polybius (ca. 160 B.C.) confirm that the tin mines of Cornwall were the source of the world's supply, exported by the Phoenicians. Diodorus Siculus gives a detailed description of the tin trade (Ref. 11:19) and Jowett states that:

> The association of Joseph of Arimathea with the tin industry in Cornwall is positive. Fragments of poems and miners' songs, handed down through the centuries, make frequent reference to Joseph. It has long been customary for the miners to shout when they worked, "Joseph was a tin man," "Joseph was in the tin trade." These were their chief trade slogans which identified Joseph as a prominent person in the British tin industry. (Ref. 18:43)

At the time of Christ, Joseph is supposed to have controlled a major portion of the tin trade, and owned a large estate about eight miles north of Jerusalem at Arimathaea, known today as Ramalleh, on the caravan route between Nazareth and Jerusalem. (Ref. 18:17-18)

Events concerning Joseph of Arimathaea recorded in the Bible and discussed subsequently are given added clarity when the relationship of Joseph to Jesus is considered. The following two quotations attest that Joseph was related to Jesus. The first quotation claims that Joseph was the younger brother of the father of Mary, while the second claims that Joseph was the next male kin of the husband. The important point is that Joseph may have been a close relative to Jesus.

> Ancient traditions, in the Eastern Church, assert that Joseph was the great-uncle of Jesus. This is confirmed by the Jewish Talmud which has Joseph as the younger

brother of the father of Mary and thus was her uncle and
a great-uncle to Jesus. The Harlei[a]n Manuscripts (in
the British Museum—38-59 f, 193 b) further supports
this claim that Joseph of Arimathaea was uncle to the
Blessed Mary. (Ref. 7:19)

During the lifetime of Jesus there constantly appears
reference to his association with a relative at Jerusalem.
Profane history is more positive on the matter, identifying the connection with Joseph. As we study the old
records we find there is a valid reason for the close association of Jesus and his family with Joseph. It is quite obvious that the husband of Mary died while Jesus was
young. Under Jewish law such a circumstance automati-
cally appointed the next male kin of the husband, in this
case Joseph, legal guardian of the family. This fact
explains many things. History and tradition report Jesus,
as a boy, frequently in the company of His uncle, particu-
larly at the time of the religious feasts. (Ref. 18:18)

JESUS AT THE TEMPLE

Jesus went with his parents to Jerusalem to the Feast
of the Passover when he was twelve years old. After the
feast, his parents,

> ...supposing him to have been in the company, went a
> day's journey; and they sought him among their kinsfolk
> and acquaintance. And when they found him not, they
> turned back again to Jerusalem, seeking him. And it
> came to pass, that after three days they found him in the
> temple, sitting in the midst of the doctors, both hearing
> them, and asking them questions. (Luke 2:44-46)

Significant are the facts that they traveled a "day's journey" without missing Jesus, and then they "sought him among their kinsfolk." Several authors have concluded that in Jerusalem they were at the town home of their uncle Joseph, and that after a day's journey of eight miles they were at Joseph's other home in Arimathaea. Hence, being among kinsfolk, they had supposed Jesus to be with other members of the family.

JESUS' MATURING YEARS

In the Joseph Smith Translation of Matthew 3: 24-26, Jesus' maturing years are briefly discussed:

> And it came to pass that Jesus grew up with his brethren, and waxed strong, and waited upon the Lord for the time of his ministry to come. And he served under his father, and he spake not as other men, neither could he be taught; for he needed not that any man should teach him. And after many years the hour of his ministry drew nigh.

This quotation indicates that at least the early years of Christ's life were spent with his brethren, working with his father, and he was self-taught and enlightened by the Holy Ghost. He possessed great knowledge of the scriptures at age 12. He had the capacity and the desire to learn by reading and by observing without the need "for any man to teach him." He quietly "waited upon the Lord for the time of his ministry to come." Hence, he lived among men without them being aware of who he was.

From these passages of scripture the conclusion cannot be drawn that he spent all of the first thirty years of his life in "the eastern part of Galilee" where his father took his family when he returned from Egypt. Except for the brief account in Matthew, the Bible is silent concerning Jesus' whereabouts from age 12 to 30.

Legends report that Jesus spent at least part of those 18 years away from Palestine. For instance, religious teachers in India have asserted that he spent three years studying there before traveling on to Tibet. Other traditions take Jesus to Egypt. But the strongest and most persistent traditions report that he spent considerable time on the Isle of Avalon at Glastonbury in southwestern England.

JESUS IN ENGLAND

The tradition of Jesus coming as a boy to Britain with Joseph of Arimathaea is found in many towns in Cornwall, Somerset and Gloucestershire in southwest England. (Ref. 11:31-33)

Legends are most tenaciously held in Cornwall, not only that Jesus was brought as a boy by Joseph, but that Jesus returned and lived at Glastonbury prior to his ministry. Even today there are homes in and around Glastonbury where an extra place is laid at the table in the belief that one day the Savior will return. (Ref. 13:13-14) C. C. Dobson lists twenty locations in southwest

England where traditions of the Lord's visits are still found.

This stanza from William Blake's poem Jerusalem has been learned and sung at schools in England with spirit and fervor for many decades:

> And did those feet in ancient times
> Walk upon England's mountains green?
> And was the holy lamb of God
> On England's pleasant pastures seen?
> And did the Countenance Divine
> Shine forth upon our clouded hills?
> And was Jerusalem builded here
> Amid these dark Satanic mills?

In England, the Savior could have found peace among friends and prepare for his forthcoming mission. Some think that he would not have spent the entire 18 years between 12 and 30 among the Jews and Romans when Satanic influence was very evident there. It may be significant that the Roman legions were never able to penetrate westward into Glastonbury. Western England including Wales, and northern England including Scotland, remained free of Roman domination. Among the questions raised by the legends and traditions of Christ's visit to Britain is the question of whether he may have also visited it as the resurrected Lord.

CHRIST'S TRIAL AND BURIAL

As a member of the Sanhedrin, Joseph of Arimathaea was probably present during at least part of the Savior's trial, but Luke 23:51 records, he "had not consented to the counsel and deed" of the Jewish leaders.

After the death of the Savior, about three in the afternoon, Joseph again comes into the story. If Jesus' body were not claimed by sundown three hours hence, the body by law would have been removed and cast into a common pit with other condemned criminals. The following day was the sabbath and "the bodies should not remain upon the cross on the sabbath day." (John 19:31) Undoubtedly, the Jews wanted to erase all identity of this enemy. (Ref. 18:22,23)

Joseph went boldly to Pilate and received permission to remove the Lord's mortal remains. Joseph and Nicodemus (who was also a member of the Sanhedrin and who had befriended Jesus early in the Savior's ministry) hurriedly anointed the body, wrapped it in linen, placed it in Joseph's own sepulchre in his nearby garden (see Figure 37), and rolled a large stone over the entrance. (Matthew 27:60)

Figure 37
Garden Tomb in Jerusalem (Ref. 7:21)

Three conclusions may be drawn from Joseph's request for the body: (1) he had to hurry to save it from being cast into a common burial pit by the authorities before the beginning of the sabbath at sundown, (2) he had the authority as a family member to do so (perhaps as the legal guardian of the Savior's mother [Ref. 19:154], since her husband had died earlier), and (3) he went boldly because he was respected by Pilate, not only because of his wealth, but also by virtue of his Roman title, Nobilis Decurio.

The Bible says nothing further about Joseph, but legends and ancient manuscripts report his going to Britain and his close associations with the Savior's apostles and disciples. (Ref. 7:21-22)

WITHOUT OARS AND SAILS

The resurrection of Christ and the subsequent success of the apostles in preaching the gospel served to further enrage the chief priests and Pharisees. The apostles scattered, but continued their effective missionary labors. Joseph of Arimathaea was a target for the vindictiveness of the chief priests and Pharisees. It is thought by some that within three years of the crucifixion, he and several close associates left Jerusalem.

Cardinal Baronius, who was considered the most outstanding historian of the Roman Catholic Church and was Curator of the Vatican Library, wrote in his Ecclesiastical Annals (1601) that in the year 36 A.D.,

Joseph of Arimathaea, Lazarus, Mary, Martha, Marcella (their maid), and Maximin (a disciple) were put in a boat without sails and without oars in the Mediterranean to die. Baronius reports that with divine help they survived, landing at Marseille. Joseph, Mary, and some others of the group traveled on to Glastonbury and Joseph died there. (Ref. 18:32-33)

> No doubt, this event in British history will come as a surprise to many Christians, but there is a mass of corroborative evidence to support this historic passage by many reliable Greek and Roman authorities, including affirmation in the Jewish Encyclopedia, under "Arles."
>
> The expulsion of Joseph and his companions in an oarless boat without sails would be in keeping with the malicious design of the Sanhedrin. They dared not openly destroy him and, instead, conceived an ulterior method hoping their ingenious treachery would eventually consign Joseph and his companions to a watery grave. Little did they realize that, by this subtle act in ridding themselves of the outstanding champion of Christ, their very hope for destruction would be circumvented by an act of providence. Their perfidy made it possible for the forgotten Fathers of Christianity to congregate in a new land where they would be free from molestation. (Ref. 18:33)

A word of explanation is needed regarding the mother of Jesus being with Joseph of Arimathaea. The apostle John at the crucifixion received the directive from Jesus to care for Jesus' mother. John undoubtedly did take and provide for her, but intense persecution and missionary labors may have prevented long-term assistance.

Jowett states that "...at no time does John refer to Mary.... [L]ack of reference to her by John could only mean one thing: the beloved Mary was not with him." (Ref. 18:133) One page earlier, Jowett makes the comment that:

> Documentary testimony, by no means British, informs us with conviction that Mary, the mother of Jesus, was an occupant of the castaway boat that arrived in Marseilles with the others before mentioned. Other reports take up the story in Gaul, attesting to the fact that Mary was a member of the Josephian Mission that arrived in Britain A.D. 36.

H. A. Lewis researched legends across Gaul in Limoges and in the Rhone Valley in France along the tin trade route concerning the presence of Joseph and the refugees as they traveled from Jerusalem to England. The name of Joseph was found in many places along the tin route. (Ref. 20:9,10)

> The Rhone Valley legends, while dealing principally with the reputed settlement there of Martha, Mary and Lazarus, mention Joseph as their "companion" in emigration, but distinctly suggest that he moves on elsewhere. Where should that be, except to his eventual legendary home at Glastonbury? (Ref. 20:10)

According to these traditions, Joseph of Arimathaea also brought with him to Glastonbury his daughter Anna, cousin to Mary the mother of Jesus. By tradition, Anna is believed to have married into the royal line from which the House of Tudor descended. (Ref. 38:205, 206-208)

JOSEPH OF ARIMATHAEA AND MARY AT GLASTONBURY

When Joseph of Arimathaea arrived, the legends say, at Glastonbury (Avalon) in England (see Figure 1 for location), with Mary the mother of Jesus and other refugees from Jerusalem, he was met by King Arviragus of the House of Siluria, the oldest royal house known in England. Joseph was known and respected here in England because of supposedly prior visits as "the tin merchant." The king bestowed on the refugees title to twelve hides of land. Each hide was 160 acres, making the total land grant 1920 acres. (Ref. 7:39-42)

According to the traditions, the teachings of Jesus brought by Joseph and the other refugees were readily accepted by Arviragus and his subjects who were already grounded in the Mosaic covenant which had been previously brought by Jeremiah. The Britons were looking forward to the coming of Christ and welcomed the gospel brought by Joseph.

A wattle church was constructed at Glastonbury about 37 A.D. which was 26 feet wide and 60 feet in length (Ref. 19:158). The church was carefully preserved later by encasing it in boards covered with lead. A stone church was erected over the encased wattle church. In 546 A. D. a large church was erected over the entire site. (Refs.

7:50; 19:158; 35:155)

Many legends also tell us that ancient records were housed at the extensive library in the Norman Church at Glastonbury. These records were quoted by numerous authors, but unfortunately the originals and the church were destroyed in a great fire in 1184 A.D. (Ref. 7:59,60)

> Despite the fierce conflicts that raged throughout Britain against Roman tyranny, Avalon [Glastonbury] was ever a safe sanctuary for apostle or neophyte. To this hallowed haven many of our Lord's original disciples came: Lazarus, Barnabas, Zaccheus, James, Luke, Simon, Paul and Peter, of whom we have positive record, leaving only three not definitely chronicled, Matthew, Mark and John, though it is recorded that at the death of Mary [about 48 A.D.] all the living original band were present at her request. (Ref. 18:171)

Joseph of Arimathaea is believed to have died at Glastonbury, Avalon, in 82 A.D. (Ref. 18:229) In 1927 researchers believed they had found Joseph's tombstone, bearing an inscription which when translated to English read: "I came to the Britons after I buried Christ, I taught, I rested." (Ref. 11:38, 39; 36:11)

OTHER SAINTS IN BRITAIN

George Jowett claims that "There is plenty of evidence to show that Peter visited Britain and Gaul several times during his lifetime, his last visit to Britain taking place before his final arrest and crucifixion in Nero's circus at Rome." (Ref. 18:174-175) Jowett discusses these visits, and Wilson adds the following, concerning visits by other apostles:

> There are authentic records that almost all (if not ALL) the apostles visited and taught in Britain. Eusebius, regarded as the father of early church history states "The Apostles passed beyond the ocean to the Isles called the Britannic Isles" and Dorotheud, Bishop of Tyre wrote that Simon Zelotes and Aristobolus visited Britain and that Aristobolus (mentioned in Romans 16 v 10) was chosen and consecrated by St. Paul as the first Bishop in Britain. There is a strong tradition that St. Paul came to Britain and actually preached on Ludgate Hill where St. Paul's Cathedral stands today. The Roman church's own eminent historian, Cardinal Baronius, Vatican librarian, discovered documents which he quotes in his Ecclesiastical Annals, listing thirteen companions of Joseph of Arimathaea, who accompanied him to Britain. This fascinating list included the Bethany sisters and their maid Marcella and brother Lazarus. (Ref. 36:11)

James H. Anderson in God's Covenant Race comments on Paul's possible visit to Spain and Britain: "St. Paul himself, writing from Corinth, tells the Romans of his intention to visit Spain." (See Romans 15:23-25; 28; Anderson reference is below) Anderson also quotes from

> ...the "long-lost chapter of Acts of the Apostles," as it has been known and spoken of for ages, discovered in the relics of the church of St. Sophia in Constantinople and

translated into English in 1801.

Here is his quotation from that chapter:

> And Paul preached mightily in Spain, and great multitudes believed and were converted, for they perceived that he was an apostle sent from God. And they departed out of Spain, and Paul and his company finding a ship in Armorica sailing unto Britain, they went therein, and passing along the south coast they reached a port called Raphinus (the modern Sandwich, Kent, England). Now when it was noised abroad that the apostle had landed on their coast, great multitudes of the inhabitants met him, and they treated Paul courteously, and he entered in at the east gate of their city, and lodged in the house of an Hebrew, and one of his own nation. And on the morrow he came and stood upon Mount Lud; and the people thronged at the gate, and assembled in the Broadway, and he preached Christ unto them, and many believed the word and the testimony of Jesus. (Ref. 1: 54)

Jowett also claims that the apostle Paul came to Britain, landing at Portsmouth in Wales in 58 A.D. (Ref. 18:192, 194) This landing could have occurred before or after the landing at Sandwich, Kent, noted above by Anderson. And Jowett accepts that Paul preached on Ludgate Hill, also known locally as Cornhill, where the famous St. Paul's Cathedral now stands.

John W. Taylor summarizes in detail the references, records, and legends concerning Joseph, Mary, and other saints in Britain. His conclusion regarding consistency is informative.

The fact that the various histories and traditions do not conflict with or contradict one another but, on the contrary, combine to substantiate the traditional journey of St. Joseph, is one which demands some explanation. ... [B]ehind these local traditions there has always existed a substream of historical fact which itself is the reason for their mutual harmony and support. (Ref. 35:176-178)

KING ARTHUR

The legendary British King Arthur, sovereign of the knights of the Round Table, may be derived from a real warrior-king who lived about 500 A.D. Traditionally, Arthur and some of his knights are claimed as direct descendants of Joseph of Arimathaea, Arthur being the eighth or ninth generation from Joseph. (Ref. 21:158-159; 19:159) Raymond Capt (Ref. 7:99) states that Arthur was tenth generation in descent. E. O. Gordon (Ref. 16) references several early documents attesting to Arthur's existence.

Standards of conduct credited to Arthur and his knights were basic Christian values. His influences and his military capability were needed to counter the advances of the pagan Saxons who were invading from the east. Once again the cradle of Christianity in Wales and in western and northern Britain was threatened.

King Arthur and Queen Guinevere were buried according to legend near the site of the Old Wattle Church at Glastonbury about 540 A.D. The graves of Arthur and Guinevere were discovered, according to the contemporary writer Gerald of Wales, in 1190 A.D. (Ref. 160-191) At the gravesite, an interesting sign reads "So ancient that only legend can record their origin."

The first serious treatment of King Arthur is Geoffrey of Monmouth's History of the Kings of Britain, brought out between 1139 and 1147 A.D. More extensive writing may have been destroyed in the fire at Glastonbury in 1184 A.D. and earlier scattered references to an Arthurian figure (and names associated with him in later chronicles) are to be found in Welsh and ecclesiastical writings.

THE REFORMATION

A modern review of significant events and times associated with the reformation era yields a surprising pattern. Over a relatively short time, a rich outpouring of divine guidance is obvious. The unfolding pattern, one event building upon another, with a consistent and growing clarification, portrays divine handiwork, which, to the Latter-day Saint, appears entirely consistent with preparations for the commencement in 1820 of the restoration of the gospel in its fullness.

John Wycliffe set the stage when he made the first translation of the Bible into medieval English about 1370 and attacked practices and dogmas of the Catholic Church. Other crucial events include these:

In 1514 Pope Paul III forbade the printing of any books without the church's permission. (Ref. 12:154)

Martin Luther completed his translation of the New Testament into German in 1522.

William Tyndale translated into "modern" English the New Testament in 1526 and the Pentateuch in 1531.

With reference to this period of history, when printing became so intertwined with social and political change, Isabel Hill Elder notes that "The Catholic Vicar of Croyden, preaching at St. Paul's Cross in the days of Henry VIII, declared that either the Roman Church must abolish printing or printing would abolish her!" (Ref. 12:154)

In about 1536, King Henry VIII broke with the Pope in Rome and established the Church of England. His successor, Edward VI, continued support for the new church, but the pro-Catholic Mary I repealed all the anti-papal legislation adopted by Henry VIII. Nevertheless, her successor, Queen Elizabeth I, completely separated Britain from the Catholic Church and restored Protestantism. She had Bibles in English placed in each parish and read each Sunday. Elizabeth made the following statement when urged to follow the Pope: "I will answer you in the words of Joshua. As Joshua said of himself and his, 'I and my realm will serve the Lord.'" (Ref. 12:156)

In 1611, the King James ("Authorized") translation of the Bible was published. Protestant Baptists had split with the Church of England about 1609, and the Methodists emerged about 1739. A new law passed in England in 1812 protected increased freedom of worship.

The continued growth of Protestantism and subsequent migrations to the New World laid the foundation for the restoration of the gospel in its fullness in preparation for the millennium. English devotional poems and hymns written between 1500 and 1850 A.D. are still sung extensively today. These hymns clearly reflect the spread and impact of true Christian doctrine.

ROYAL HOUSE OF BRITAIN

Some historians and genealogists accept that British Royalty has descended through the centuries from Hebrew and Israelite stock. Hu the Mighty and Brutus the Trojan are seen as Hebrew migrants who each ruled in his own time. The prophet Jeremiah is believed to have come to Britain with the elder daughter of the deposed King Zedekiah of the Kingdom of Judah. She, of Pharez-Judah, married the Irish King of Zarah-Judah ancestry, thus uniting the twin branches of Judah.

When, the legends continue, Joseph of Arimathaea came with his daughter Anna, a cousin of Mary the mother of Jesus, she likewise married British royalty.

According to this line of thinking, the present monarchs of Great Britain can trace their ancestry to Judah through more than one hundred generations of monarchs of Ireland, Scotland, and England. This logic raises the possibility that the scepter originally held by rulers in Jerusalem has been in the hands of the British nobility for nearly 2600 years, in literal fulfillment of ancient prophecy.

W. M. H. Milner's The Royal House of Britain, an

Enduring Dynasty (Ref. 25) details and documents the genealogical history of British Royalty. His work, first published in 1902 with the 11th edition in 1975, confirms the 1881 publication by Rev. Frederick Robert Augustus Glover. In 1908 Milner "...reading in the British Museum Library, found all Mr. Glover's authorities, as well as other valuable matter now for the first time unearthed, and went over every quotation line by line, demonstrating their correctness and the general reasonableness of Mr. Glover's conclusions." (Ref. 25:7) Figure 38 shows key ancestral lines. Milner's chart The Illustrious Lineage of the Royal House of Britain (Ref. 24) shows in detail more than 800 names of royalty from the time of Judah to Queen Elizabeth II. British royalty coupled with Ephraim's leadership have contributed greatly to maintaining the Isles of the Sea as a refuge for Israel and for Christianity.

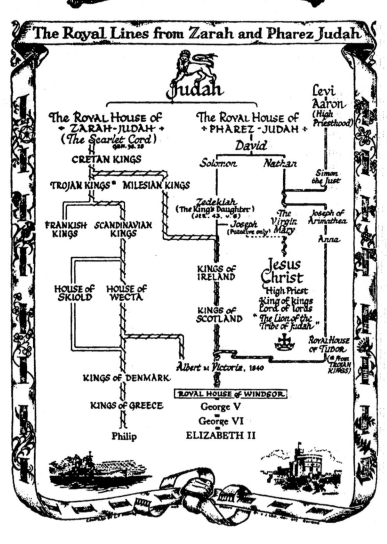

Figure 38
British Royal Ancestry (Ref. 25: 4)

CHAPTER SIX

THE RESTORATION

If we treat traditional history as historical fact, migrations from Israel to the Isles of the Sea occurred; divine guidance manifested itself throughout the centuries; the House of Israel was preserved; the reformation commenced, during which the Bible was translated and made available to the people; and the pace of recovery from darkness quickened as new freedoms were established. The power of Britain grew, and extensive colonies were established where increased freedom prevailed.

A FRONTIER PROVIDED IN AMERICA

Selected families gathered under divine guidance on the frontier of America where greater freedom from restrictive traditions existed. These were God-fearing people of simple faith, willing to listen and to be taught. When restrictive and authoritarian dominations as well as persecutions increased, those who had joined the Church of Jesus Christ of Latter-day Saints moved westward, away from tyranny and abuse where they could continue to "worship God according to the dictates of their own conscience."

PROPHETIC LEADERSHIP

Early in the 1800s, the Lord placed on stage a prophet to restore to the family of man the gospel in its fullness. It was in the morning of a beautiful clear day, early in the spring of 1820. The young Joseph Smith, whose ancestors had immigrated to the United States from Britain, knelt in humble prayer in upper New York and asked for divine guidance. His prayer was answered. On April 6, 1830 the Church of Jesus Christ of Latter-day Saints was organized.

Since that time, a rich outpouring of divine communication has occurred. The sixth and last dispensation is underway. With the gospel in its fullness being revealed, the gathering of Israel could commence. (Ref. 31:4-8)

GATHERING OF ISRAEL

The dispersion and subsequent gathering of Israel were and are world-wide endeavors. The Lord made these predictions through the prophet Amos. "For, lo, I will command, and I will sift the house of Israel among all nations." (Amos 9:9) The gathering is to be from the isles of the sea, from the north countries, and from all countries, as the Lord said, "where I had driven them." (See Jeremiah 23:8; 2 Nephi 10:8)

GATHERING OF EPHRAIM

Ephraim received the birthright for all of Israel from his grandfather Jacob. Joshua, an Ephraimite, led the Israelites into Palestine following the Exodus. Ephraim was the leader of the Ten Tribes of Israel. Now, leadership for the restoration of the gospel comes also from the tribe of Ephraim.

Blessings given by latter-day patriarchs have confirmed that the prophet Joseph Smith was an Ephraimite as were all of the leaders of the newly organized Church of Jesus Christ of Latter-day Saints. All of them had their roots in Britain. They or their parents or grandparents had emigrated from Britain. And all subsequent presidents of the restored church trace their lineage to the British Isles. For more than one hundred and fifty years, missionaries gathered descendants of Ephraim from the four corners of the world.

Shortly after the church was organized in 1830, Canada and England became the first countries to receive missionaries. It is significant that the first missionaries to go abroad went to England in 1837 to the northwest coast where, the legends tell us, faithful Christians had sought refuge from Roman and pagan invasions.

When missionaries from America arrived in Preston, England, a parliamentary election was underway, called by the young Queen Victoria. The missionaries' attention was caught by the unrolling of an election banner with the motto "Truth Will Prevail." "So powerful was the impression upon the elders that they took this slogan as the motto for their own work in Britain." (Ref. 5:73)

Their efforts met with phenomenal success. Apostle Heber C. Kimball in his journal records that a remarkable outpouring of the Spirit occurred in the small villages of Chatburn and Dunham in the Ribble Valley near Preston. When the prophet Joseph Smith was informed of the occasion, he responded that ancient prophets had been to the area and had blessed the land.

Derek A. Cuthbert shares the belief that the British Isles have been favored of the Lord with a divine destiny: "Yes, the Blood of Israel is richly concentrated in these islands and the promised blessings will all be fulfilled." (Ref. 10:194)

The remarkable success of Apostle Wilford Woodruff in 1840 with the United Brethren living near Ledbury in Herefordshire, England is indicative of the people's preparation before his coming. All but one of the six hundred United Brethren readily accepted the restored gospel. And in eight months of missionary effort in the counties of Hereford, Gloucester and Worcester, eighteen hundred souls were baptized. (Ref. 14:114)

At one time in the 1850s, there were nearly three times as many members of the newly founded church in Britain than there were in North America. Patriarchal blessings indicate that most of these were Ephraimites.

SOME WERE NOT RECEPTIVE

In August 1840, three apostles (Wilford Woodruff, Heber C. Kimball, and George P. Smith) went to "...the great city of London, the largest, most noted and populous commercial city in the world, with a population of about one million five hundred thousand people" at the time. (Ref. 5:150) These were the same apostles who had such remarkable success during the previous months.

On September 9 Wilford Woodruff wrote in his journal the following harsh appraisal of the receptiveness of the people in London to their message, this in stark contrast to their prior success in the Preston and Herefordshire areas. "We had spent twenty-three days in great Babylon of modern times and had found it harder to establish the Church there than in any other place we had ever been. We [3 able apostles] had baptized one man." (Ref. 5:155; 14:171) By October 13, after about two months of intensive effort, they had baptized eleven only. They stated that

> ...in our travels, either in America or Europe, we have never before found a people from whose minds we have had to remove a greater multiplicity of objections or combinations of obstacles, in order to excite an interest in the subject and prepare the heart for the reception of the word of God, than in the city of London. (Ref. 14:173)

It seems very possible from these strikingly different experiences that the elect of Israel were not in the worldly city of London, and that wealth and materialism had diverted people's attention from spiritual values: they may not have been prepared by ancient prophets. Possibly, by this time, London may have been a largely unreceptive (gentile?) community.

RETURN OF THE LOST TRIBES

Four basic questions concerning the "lost tribes" of Israel must be asked: Who are they? Where are they? When will they return? How will they return? The recorded words of the prophets shed light upon these questions, but do not provide definitive answers.

WHO ARE THE LOST TRIBES?

In Matthew 10:6, Christ sent his apostles to "the lost sheep of the house of Israel." Later, in Matthew 15:24 he said "I am not sent but unto the lost sheep of the house of Israel." And in John 10:16, as already discussed in Chapter 3, he said "And other sheep I have, which are not of this fold: them also I must bring, and they shall hear my voice; and there shall be one fold, and one shepherd."

As the resurrected Lord, Jesus Christ came to the Nephites on the American continent. He stated there that his coming was in fulfillment of his statement to his apostles in Jerusalem that he would go to the lost sheep of Israel. As he was leaving the Nephites, he said "But now

I go unto the Father, and also to show myself unto the lost tribes of Israel" (3 Nephi 17:4), indicating that there were other "lost sheep" than the "American" branch of transplanted Israelites he was then visiting. Who were these other lost sheep? One would anticipate that if he had visited any of the scattered of Israel in Britain or Scandinavia or Netherlands, the impact would be evidence, and at least that legends would have persisted as they have among the Indians of America. Today the American Indians in North and South America speak many different languages, but they have retained a cultural tradition of the Great White God who gave them so much of value. Northern Europeans have no such tradition of a visit by the resurrected Christ. But residents in southwest England have retained the tradition of the visit of the boy Jesus, brought by his uncle Joseph of Arimathaea, as discussed earlier.

On this subject, Ernest L. Whitehead quotes Mr. A. R. Heaver, English publicist, who states:

> The tradition that our Lord visited Glastonbury (Somerset, England) is very strong in the west of England, but it is an oral tradition only. ... [Nevertheless,] Gildas, a British historian in 642 A.D. says "We know that Christ, the true Son, afforded his light to our island in the last year of the reign of Tiberius Caesar." This would place the date at from A.D. 34 to A.D. 38, a date that conforms very accurately with that of Christ's crucifixion, and later visitations among the Jews and Nephites. (Ref. 38:167)

Today we look forward to the time when additional
scriptures will be available, detailing the visits of the resurrected Christ to Lost Israel.

WHERE ARE THE LOST TRIBES?

> Behold, I will bring them from the north country, and
> gather them from the coasts of the earth.... (Jeremiah
> 31:8)
>
> Yea, then will he remember the isles of the sea; yea,
> and all the people who are of the house of Israel, will I
> gather in, saith the Lord, according to the words of the
> prophet Zenos, from the four quarters of the earth. (1
> Nephi 19:16)
>
> And it shall come to pass that they shall be gathered
> in from their long dispersion, from the isles of the sea,
> and from the four parts of the earth; and the nations of
> the Gentiles shall be great in the eyes of me, saith God, in
> carrying them forth to the lands of their inheritance. (2
> Nephi 10:8)
>
> Ho, ho, come forth, and flee from the land of the
> north, saith the LORD: for I have spread you abroad as
> the four winds of the heaven, saith the LORD. (Zechariah
> 2;6)
>
> In those days the house of Judah shall walk with the
> house of Israel, and they shall come together out of the
> land of the north to the land that I have given for an
> inheritance unto your fathers. (Jeremiah 3:18)

The scriptures quoted above appear to use three distinctively different terms to describe the location of lost

and scattered Israel:

1. Four quarters of the earth, parts of the earth, nations
   of the Gentiles, coasts of the earth, and all the lands
   where he had driven them;
2. Isles of the sea;
3. North country, countries, and land of the north.

The first category might refer to those who had been broadly scattered over the earth, the second category to those primarily in Britain and America, and the third category to those north of Jerusalem in western Asia and eastern Europe. Will the remnant spoken of as the lost ten tribes return as a body out of those north countries after they have been given the restored gospel?

Traditions exist which link remnants of the ten tribes to northern and eastern Europe and western Asia. Archeological evidence suggests many migrations from the Near East which might trace the movements of migrating Israelites. Linguistic evidence also links the languages of inhabitants of these lands to Hebrew language characteristics.

But what about the main body of the Ten Tribes? Did the dispersion, the scattering, prophesied for Israel involve all or did some tribes remain intact, still existing as an organized body today? James H. Anderson (Ref. 1:114-116) discusses in depth and strongly criticizes theories at one time widely believed that the lost tribes were together either in the north polar regions or in the middle of the earth. He finds both theories unreasonable.

WHEN AND HOW WILL THE LOST TRIBES RETURN?

The most detailed statement regarding the coming forth of the lost tribes was given by the Lord in 1831:

> And they who are in the north countries shall come in remembrance before the Lord; and their prophets shall hear his voice, and shall no longer stay themselves; and they shall smite the rocks, and the ice shall flow down at their presence. And an highway shall be cast up in the midst of the great deep. Their enemies shall become a prey unto them, And in the barren deserts there shall come forth pools of living water; and the parched ground shall no longer be a thirsty land. And they shall bring forth their rich treasures unto the children of Ephraim, my servants. And the boundaries of the everlasting hills shall tremble at their presence. And there shall they fall down and be crowned with glory, even in Zion, by the hands of the servants of the Lord, even the children of Ephraim. And they shall be filled with songs of everlasting joy. Behold, this is the blessing of the everlasting God upon the tribes of Israel, and the richer blessing upon the head of Ephraim and his fellows. And they also of the tribe of Judah, after their pain, shall be sanctified in holiness before the Lord, to dwell in his presence day and night, forever and ever. (D & C 133:26-35)

Several statements in this prophecy suggest when and how the lost tribes of Israel will return. However, as with most prophecies, these statements may be allegorical rather than literal only. Might it be so with the prophecy of "ice flowing down," casting up a "highway in the great deep" and bringing forth "rich treasures"? Does the light of the gospel not melt the ice of darkness and does the hand of the Lord not melt opposition (dissolving the Soviet Union and removing the Berlin Wall, for instance)? Were those early converts from Britain provided a highway across the ocean by the Perpetual Emigration Fund, even though many had not the monetary resources to book passage? None were left behind who desired to flee to Zion. And did they not bring their treasures with them, sufficient to build the Kirtland Temple, where glorious events transpired? And did they not provide rich ancestral ties through which eternal blessings could flow to those who followed them?

Another hypothesis might also be considered. Has the return of the lost tribes of Israel been underway for many years as an evolving and sequential process? And might we expect a dramatic conclusion when the gospel is carried to the remaining tribes, those thought to be in eastern and northern Europe and western Asia, as the Holy Ghost testifies to them and they begin to come forth?

Eventually, the events named in the prophecies will occur as stated, but looking ahead we cannot say with certainty when or how. Nevertheless, the unfolding panorama will always be an exciting one as long-sought answers to the questions of who, where, when, and how are clearly illuminated.

JOHN THE REVELATOR

Through the question-and-answer format of D & C 77:14, we learn that the apostle John was assigned the spiritual mission of the gathering or unifying of the Twelve Tribes in the last days.

According to John Whitmer's History of the Church (Ch. 5), the prophet Joseph Smith revealed in June 1831

> that John the Revelator was then among the Ten Tribes of Israel who had been led away by Shalmaneser, King of Assyria, to prepare them for their return from their long dispersion, to again possess the land of their fathers.

This revelation is significant. John's mission was important and timely, since within only six years (by 1837) apostles would be bringing the restored gospel to the inhabitants of Britain. History records that many in Britain were ready to a remarkable degree. It is believed that those to whom the apostles brought the gospel were mainly of Ephraim. Since Ephraim was the ordained leader of Israel, it is reasonable to assert that the royal blood of Ephraim comprised the initial leadership of the restoration.

Ephraim's gathering has been underway for more than 150 years, and Ephraim has built the temples and administered the ordinances. Ephraim, as the birthright holder and thereby the leader of Israel, has provided unified leadership for the return of lost Israel. The next phase of the gathering will be for the prophets of Ephraim to direct the carrying of the gospel to the remaining tribes, and to lead them forth out of obscurity to Zion.

GATHERING OF JUDAH

The prophetic language of Isaiah 11:12 states that the Lord will "...gather together the dispersed of Judah from the four corners of the earth." That gathering has been occurring and was given official status in 1948 when Israel became a republic. Judah's enemies have repeatedly tried to destroy the Republic of Israel and to prevent the gathering, but miracles have occurred and the gathering continues.

The conversion of the main body of the Tribe of Judah to the restored gospel of Jesus Christ will not occur until the resurrected Savior has appeared on the Mount of Olives. The gathering of the other Tribes of Israel will be essentially complete before Judah accepts the restored gospel: Christ said frequently that the first shall be last and the last shall be first.

CHAPTER SEVEN

GOD'S COVENANT ISRAEL

Moses speaking to the Israelites made a profound statement: "For thou art an holy people unto the Lord thy God; the Lord thy God hath chosen thee to be a special people unto himself, above all people that are upon the face of the earth." (Deuteronomy 7:6) Judah and Ephraim, two of the twelve tribes of Israel, also received special blessings.

JUDAH'S BLESSING

Judah was blessed with the sceptre. "The sceptre shall not depart from Judah, nor a lawgiver from between his feet, until Shiloh [Christ] come." (Genesis 49:10) David and Solomon reigned and prophets wrote, and from Judah has come the Bible preparing the people for the restoration of the gospel in its fullness.

The sceptre was taken from the Jews in Jerusalem in fulfillment of Jesus' proclamation to the chief priests: "The kingdom of God shall be taken from you, and given to a nation bringing forth the fruits thereof." (Matthew 21:43)

EPHRAIM'S BLESSING

Ephraim, the son of Joseph, received the birthright, the leadership blessing for all of Israel. Jacob in his blessing to his son Joseph said:

> Joseph is a fruitful bough, even a fruitful bough by a well; whose branches run over the wall. ... The blessings of thy father have prevailed above the blessings of my progenitors unto the utmost bound of the everlasting hills: they shall be on the head of Joseph, and on the crown of the head of him that was separate from his brethren. (Genesis 49: 22, 26)

Joseph's branches ran over the wall when a "bough" of his posterity took their families to America, from whom came the Book of Mormon, holy scriptures providing another witness of the divinity and mission of Jesus Christ.

The posterity of Joseph's son Ephraim is giving prophetic leadership from the everlasting hills to the restoration of the gospel in its fullness, and to the gathering of Israel, as prophesied in Isaiah 11:12: "And he shall set up an ensign for the nations, and shall assemble the outcasts of Israel, and gather together the dispersed of Judah from the four corners of the earth." Erastus Snow in 1882 made the following prophetic statement regarding the seed of Ephraim:

> And when books shall be opened and the lineage of all men is known, it will be found that they have been first

and foremost in everything noble among men in the various nations in breaking off the shackles of kingcraft and priestcraft and oppression of every kind, and the foremost among men in upholding and maintaining the principles of liberty and freedom upon this continent [America] and establishing a representative government, and thus preparing the way for the coming forth of the fullness of the everlasting gospel. (as quoted in Ref. 2:49)

EPHRAIM AND JUDAH WORKING TOGETHER

Interesting insights into the unique and supportive role of Ephraim and Judah are given by David—"Ephraim also is the strength of mine head; Judah is my lawgiver" (Psalms 60:7)—and by Isaiah: "The envy also of Ephraim shall depart, and the adversaries of Judah shall be cut off: Ephraim shall not envy Judah, and Judah shall not vex Ephraim." (Isaiah 11:13) The statements of David and Isaiah are graphically portrayed in Figure 30 (the British Royal Arms) where the two kingdoms of Israel represented by the Lion of Judah and the Unicorn of Ephraim are supporting the shield of Britain.

The spiritual history we are trying to trace in this book asserts that together Judah and Ephraim have built Great Britain. From that heritage sprang colonies worldwide, and today the strength of democracy and Christianity lies within gathered Israel, comprising Great Britain and her former colonies, especially the United States of America and Canada.

A DIVINE DESTINY

The hand of the Almighty has been clearly evident through the centuries. The dispersion of Israel occurred under prophetic guidance, and the fathering proceeded under prophetic guidance as well.

This book has discussed some of the traditional material which traces periodic migrations of the elect of Israel to Britain over some several thousand years. These migrating people had the gospel taught to them by prophets. They survived repeated onslaughts of the adversary because of divine protection, and Britain became the cradle from which their Christian principles were spread. Their posterity have conveyed the doctrines of freedom and good will to all men everywhere.

The great British leader, Sir Winston Churchill, said in 1942 while World War II was raging:

> I have a feeling sometimes that some Guiding Hand has interfered. I have a feeling that we have a Guardian because we have a great Cause, and we shall have that Guardian so long as we serve that Cause faithfully. And what a Cause it is. (Ref. 9:233)

The Bishop of Chelmsford, England, Dr. H. A. Wilson, also recognized the hand of God in the events of 1945:

> If ever a great nation was on the point of supreme and final disaster, and yet was saved and reinstated, it was ourselves. That is a fact which should be written on the souls of us all in indelible letters of fire. It does not

require an exceptional religious mind to detect in all this
the hand of God. It has been a miracle and the person
who does not recognize that is impervious to the deeper
significance of events. We have been saved for a purpose.
Let that be acknowledged, and it will be an immense
steadying force in our character. Our Empire has a mission to discharge to the world. That may sound old fash-
ioned and jingoistic, but it is true. (Ref. 9:233)

After World War II, President Truman, in a speech at
Washington, D.C. on April 3, 1951, expressed his belief
that the United States has a divinely appointed mission:

I do not think that anyone can study the history of
this nation of ours without becoming convinced that
Divine Providence has played a great part in it. I have a
feeling that God has created us and brought us to our
present position of power and strength for some great
purpose. It is not given to us to know fully what that purpose is. But I think we may be sure of one thing. And that
is that our country is intended to do all it can, in coopera-
tion with other nations, to help to create peace and pre-
serve peace in the world. It is given to us to defend the
spiritual values—the moral code—against the vast forces
of evil that seek to destroy them. (Ref. 9:233-234)

Queen Elizabeth II at a joint session of the American
Congress in 1991 ended her message with the humble
petition "May God bless America."

OUR RESPONSIBILITY

These noble ancestors, covenant Israel, were guided, preserved, and enlightened. We, their posterity, have an awesome responsibility. In our hands is the final dispensation, preparing the way for the return of the Christ and the ushering in of the Millennium.

Knowing whence we came provides understanding and strength to fulfill our assigned tasks. May we ever be grateful for our noble ancestors.

REFERENCES

1. James H. Anderson. God's Covenant Race (Salt Lake City, Utah: Paragon Press, Inc.), 1956.
2. Howard H. Barron. Judah, Past and Future (Bountiful, Utah: Horizon Publishers and Distributors), 1979.
3. Archibald F. Bennett. "The Children of Ephraim," Genealogical Magazine, Vol. 21 (1930), p. 67.
4. W. H. Bennett. Symbols of our Celto-Saxon Heritage (Windsor, Ontario: Herald Press Limited), 1985.
5. Ben V. Bloxham; James R. Moss; and Larry C. Porter, editors. Truth Will Prevail (Cambridge: The University Press), 1987.
6. E. Raymond Capt. Stonehenge and Druidism (Thousand Oaks, California: Artisan Sales), 1983.
7. E. Raymond Capt. The Traditions of Glastonbury (Thousand Oaks, California: Artisan Sales), 1983.
8. E. Raymond Capt. Study in Pyramidology (Thousand Oaks, California: Artisan Sales), 1986.
9. Michael A. Clark. "A Sense of Nationhood, the Great and Urgent Need," Wake Up, Vol. 7, No. 10 (Ayrshire Scotland: Christian Israel Foundation, July-August 1989), p. 232.
10. Derek A. Cuthbert. The Second Century: Latter-day Saints in Great Britain, 1937-87 (Cambridge: The University Press), 1987.
11. C. C. Dobson. Did Our Lord Visit Britain as They

Say in Cornwall and Somerset? (London:
Covenant Publishing Co., Ltd.), 1986.

12. Isabel Hill Elder. Celt, Druid and Culdee (London:
The covenant Publishing Co., Ltd.), 1986.

13. Isabel Hill Elder. Joseph of Arimathea
(Glastonbury, England: Real Israel Press), 1988.

14. Richard L. Evans. A Century of Mormonism in
Great Britain (Salt Lake City, Utah: Publishers
Press), 1937.

15. W. H. Fasken. Israel's Racial Origin and
Migrations (London: The Covenant Publishing
Co., Ltd.), 1934.

16. E. O. Gordon. Prehistoric London: Its Mounds and
Circles (London: The Covenant Publishing Co.,
Ltd.), 1985.

17. Anthony W. Ivins. "Israel in History and
Genealogy," Utah Genealogical and Historical
Magazine, Vol. 23 (Salt Lake City, Utah; January
1932).

18. George F. Jowett. The Drama of the Lost Disciples
(London: The Covenant Publishing Co., Ltd.),
1980.

19. J. O. Kinnaman. Diggers for Facts: The Bible in
the Light of Archaeology (Haverhill,
Massachusetts: Destiny Publishers), 1940.

20. H. A. Lewis. Christ in Cornwall (Salmouth,
England: J. H. Lake & Co., Ltd.), n.d.

21. Lionel Smithett Lewis. St. Joseph of Arimathea at
Glastonbury (Cambridge: James Clark & Co.,
Ltd.), 1982.

22. Nick Mann. Glastonbury Tor: A Guide to the History and Legends (England: Annenterprise), 1986.

23. Bruce R. McConkie. Mormon Doctrine (Salt Lake City, Utah: Bookcraft Publishers), 1966.

24. M. H. Milner. The Illustrious Lineage of the Royal House of Britain (London: The Covenant Publishing Co., Ltd.), 1977.

25. M. H. Milner. The Royal House of Britain: An Enduring Dynasty (Rochester, Kent: Stanhope Press [Staples Printers Ltd.]), 1975.

26. Hugh Nibley. "The World of the Jaredites," The Improvement Era (Salt Lake City, Utah), 1951.

27. W. H. Poole. History: The True Key to Prophecy (Brooklyn, New York: George W. Greenwood), 1880.

28. Andrew Rafferty and Kevin Crossley-Holland. The Stones Remain: Megalithic Sites of Britain (London: Century Hutchinson, Ltd.), 1989.

29. George Reynolds. Are We of Israel? (Salt Lake City, Utah: Deseret Sunday School Union), 1916.

30. LeGrand Richards. Israel! Do You Know? (Salt Lake City, Utah: Deseret Book Co.), 1954.

31. B. H. Roberts, editor. History of the Church of Jesus Christ of Latter-day Saints, Vol. 1 (Salt Lake City, Utah: Deseret Book Co.), 1946.

32. L. G. A. Roberts. Druidism in Britain (Vancouver, British Columbia: The Association of the Covenant People), n.d.

33. L. G. A. Roberts. "Migrations into Britain" [a map]

(London: The Covenant Publishing Co., Ltd.), n.d.

34. James E. Talmage. The Articles of Faith (Salt
    Lake City, Utah: Church of Jesus Christ of Latter-
    day Saints), 1947.

35. John W. Taylor. The Coming of the Saints
    (Thousand Oaks, California: Artisan Sales), 1985.

36. George N. Wilson. Coincidences? Pointers to our
    Heritage (Wigan: Committee of North West
    British Israel World Federation), n.d.

37. William Whiston, translator. The Complete Works
    of Josephus (Grand Rapids, Michigan: Kregal
    Publications), 1981.

38. Ernest L. Whitehead. The House of Israel
    (Independence, Missouri: Zion Printing and
    Publishing Co.), 1947.

SUPPLEMENTARY REFERENCES

39. Peter Kemp. The Campaign of the Spanish
    Armada (Oxford, England: Facts on File
    Publications), 1988.

40. H. G. Wells. The Outline of History, 2 Vols. (New
    York: Doubleday & Co., 1971 ed.), Vol. 1, p. 142.